A WORLD IN TRANSITION

FINDING SPIRITUAL SECURITY IN TIMES OF CHANGE

PARAMAHANSA YOGANANDA

— ALSO —

SRI DAYA MATA   TARA MATA

MRINALINI MATA   BROTHER ANANDAMOY

AND OTHERS

Self-Realization Fellowship
FOUNDED 1920
Paramahansa Yogananda

ABOUT THIS BOOK: Many years before the global changes that are being felt as our world moves into a new millennium, Paramahansa Yogananda, founder of Self-Realization Fellowship, described the transformations we are now undergoing. His vision for the all-round progress and well-being of individuals and nations during these times was set forth in his writings and in numerous talks given at Self-Realization Fellowship temples, which were printed in *Self-Realization* magazine and in several volumes of his collected talks and essays published by Self-Realization Fellowship. Drawing from all these sources, this compilation brings together his wisdom on the challenges and opportunities to be encountered over the decades to come, as well as contemporary discussions of this aspect of his teachings by Sri Daya Mata, current president of SRF, and other long-time monastic disciples of Paramahansa Yogananda.

Authorized by the International Publications Council of
SELF-REALIZATION FELLOWSHIP
3880 San Rafael Avenue
Los Angeles, California 90065-3298

The Self-Realization Fellowship name and emblem (shown above) appear on all SRF books, recordings, and other publications, assuring the reader that a work originates with the society established by Paramahansa Yogananda and faithfully conveys his teachings.

ISBN 0-87612-015-X
Library of Congress Catalog Card Number 99-71254
Printed in the United States of America
12853-54321

CONTENTS

"THE ONLY ANSWER IS A SPIRITUAL ONE"

BY DR. ROBERT MULLER

[Dr. Muller wrote the following as part of his Foreword to the Fiftieth Anniversary Edition of Paramahansa Yogananda's best-known work, Autobiography of a Yogi. *The excerpts below are reprinted here because Dr. Muller's words so beautifully express the hope and inspiration Paramahansa Yogananda's message conveys as we enter the new millennium.—Editor]*

One day more than thirty years ago, during the early 1960s, my American secretary at the United Nations gave to me as a birthday gift a copy of *Autobiography of a Yogi.* It was the first book by a Hindu sage I had ever read. I was fascinated by it. That copy is still with me, underlined in many places....[It] helped me enormously at the United Nations. It enabled me to view problems with the

---

Dr. Robert Muller is former United Nations Assistant Secretary-General. He is Chancellor, UN University for Peace, Costa Rica, and the author of many books, including What War Taught Me About Peace, Most of All They Taught Me Happiness, New Genesis: Shaping a Global Spirituality, *and* 2000 Ideas and Dreams for a Better World.

proper perspective, to put each one in its rightful place — on the planet, in the universe, and in time — and to approach it with a spiritual mind-set.

During one of the last years of his mandate, the former UN Secretary-General Dag Hammarskjöld said, "We have tried to make peace on this earth and we have failed miserably. Unless there is a spiritual renaissance, this world will know no peace." I grew up in Alsace-Lorraine on the border between France and Germany; my grandparents knew three wars and changed nationality five times without ever leaving their village. When I joined the United Nations international service in 1948, as a young man who had seen the most horrible atrocities of war and destruction, I was very pessimistic: If such hatred and destruction could happen between two countries that share a common civilization, how could I expect that white and black countries, rich and poor nations, thousands of religious and ethnic groups all over the world, would be able to live together in peace?

The only answer, I came to understand, is a spiritual one. During almost forty years at the United Nations, I saw one Secretary-General after another either be or become a spiritual being. Trygve Lie, the first Secretary-General, created the meditation room at the United Nations, the first meditation room in any political organization on this earth. Dag Hammarskjöld came to his post as a rational economist and ended up as one of the great mystics of our time, one who had a constant dialogue with God. U Thant, the Buddhist Secretary-General — whom I thought of as a saint in the UN — taught us that as human beings we all have physical qualities, mental qualities, moral and sentimental qualities, but that the highest quality of all is spirituality. He showed me the importance of living a spiritual life from morning to evening and not limiting it to one hour in church on Sunday.

The hope I gained from these great men and my exposure through *Autobiography of a Yogi* to the ideal of both an individual and a global spirituality has profoundly changed my outlook — so much so, in fact, that the secretary who gave me the book came into my office at the UN one day and placed on my desk a plaque engraved with the words: Robert Muller, Chief Cosmic Optimist!

As we enter a new century, a new millennium, I pray that the spirit and teachings of Paramahansa Yogananda will bless every reader with a similar rebirth of hope, and beautiful enlightenments of heart and mind, thus contributing to an evolutionary advance of humanity into a global spiritual age. How wonderful and powerful it would be if, when all delegates to the United Nations stand up in the General Assembly Hall at the beginning of each session to observe a minute of silence for prayer and meditation, at the same time all peoples of the world would pray for these representatives of the different nations, giving them the strength and divine spirit to solve many of the intractable problems facing humanity today. We might then begin to see the ideal world envisioned by Paramahansa Yogananda. As he so eloquently writes in his autobiography, a truly spiritual understanding among people and nations is urgently needed if that better and nobler world is to come into being:

> The grim march of world political events points inexorably to the truth that without spiritual vision, the people perish. Science, if not religion, has awakened in humanity a dim sense of the insecurity and even insubstantiality of all material things. Where indeed may man go now, if not to his Source and Origin, the Spirit within him?... Let nations ally themselves no longer with death, but with life; not with destruction, but with construction; not with hate, but with the creative miracles of love.

It is the spiritual dimension of life that is the highest, deepest, most universal and unifying dimension of all. [Paramahansa Yogananda's] book is truly an ambassador of light, illumining the eternal ideals that have ever been our surest guide on the path of life. It is those high and noble ideals that have helped humanity thus far to survive in this mysterious universe, and that will lead us rightly into the coming millennium. May it be the first millennium of peace and spirituality in all human history. So help us God.

Ciudad Colón, Costa Rica
December 1996

TOWARD THE MILLENNIUM

The world will go on like this in its ups and downs. Where shall we look for a sense of direction? Not to the prejudices roused within us by our habits and the environmental influences of our families, our country, or the world; but to the guiding voice of Truth within.

—*Paramahansa Yogananda*

In these pages, the visionary wisdom of one of the most revered spiritual leaders of our time sheds a clarifying light on present and future global concerns. Paramahansa Yogananda's farseeing guidance for these times of change, first articulated by him more than fifty years ago, along with contemporary discussions of his vision by his foremost living disciple, Sri Daya Mata, and other longtime monks and nuns of Self-Realization Fellowship, reframes the problems we face in a spiritual context of reassuring hope and encouragement.

The current era is one of profound changes in world civilization. Paramahansa Yogananda's guru, Swami Sri Yukteswar [1855–1936], revealed in his book, *The Holy Science,* that the Atomic Age (Dwapara Yuga) is a new ascending stage in the life of our planet. We are destined to witness far-reaching modifications in the religious, social, economic, and political institutions of humanity.*

---

* The *yugas,* or world cycles described in scriptures of India, are explained in more detail on pages 8-14.

Throughout history, there have been periods of foreboding giving rise to predictions about forthcoming natural or manmade catastrophic events. The advent of a new millennium — or, in olden times, of a descending inauspicious *yuga* (cycle)— have typically been catalysts for such pronouncements. During his lifetime, whenever Paramahansa Yogananda was questioned about negative predictions, his response was always one of optimistic faith in the will of God; and, when warranted, advice that people take whatever outward measures were practical and feasible in the circumstances. He confided to a few close disciples that God had shown him in *samadhi* (the state of God-union in deep meditation) much of the pattern of humanity's future. Though he often spoke about the general pattern of the decades to come, the great teacher refrained from making detailed public prophecies about such subjects — stressing that our planet's destiny could be modified at any time by people's exercise of their soul powers of free will, positive thinking, and faith in God. Through these means, he repeatedly affirmed, it is *always* within our power to put our lives in tune with divine harmony and healing.

For the years ahead, Paramahansa Yogananda predicted great ups and downs in the fortunes of societies and nations and thereafter a period of unparalleled progress the world over. This anthology focuses on the nature of these changes, how they will affect our lives, and what we can do about it. It is our hope that the selections herein, by identifying the universal principles that influence the evolution of civilizations and individuals, will help each reader to develop the life skills we need to chart our course as the world makes its transition into a higher age.

While the specific mission of Paramahansa Yogananda was to introduce the spiritual science of Kriya Yoga, an ancient system of meditation techniques for achieving personal experience of the Divine, which is discussed in more detail in several of the articles in this book, he honored all religions and held in respect sincere seekers of all paths to God. Many of the talks and lectures included in this book were originally given to audiences familiar with the Self-Realization Fellowship path of Kriya Yoga, and reflect the terminology of that tradition.* But the all-inclusive truths they present are applicable by anyone, of any faith, who believes that the world's true hope for peace and prosperity lies in embracing universal principles of spirituality and the oneness of all humanity. Thus can each of us meet the challenges of the new millennium not with fear, but with a positive sense of faith, strength, and inner direction to grasp to the fullest the opportunities that accompany this ascending age.

---

* Many followers of the Self-Realization Fellowship path refer to Paramahansa Yogananda by the title *guru,* or its closest English equivalent, *master.* The real meaning of the word *guru* is sometimes lost sight of. Today it is commonly misused to refer simply to a teacher or instructor. But a true, God-illumined guru is one who, in his attainment of self-mastery, has realized his identity with the omnipresent Spirit. Such a one is uniquely qualified to lead the seeker on his or her inward journey toward God-union and liberation.

PART I:

THE NEW MILLENNIUM: END OR BEGINNING?

The End of the World

Guidance and Encouragement for the Years Ahead

Are We Really Entering a Better Age?

Be Nourished by the Soul

Understanding is the most precious possession of each soul. It is your inner vision, the intuitive faculty by which you can clearly perceive the truth—about yourself and others, and all situations that arise in your path—and correctly adjust your attitudes and actions accordingly....

In this world, our understanding is often short-sighted. When our mental vision is thus impaired, it is impossible to see into the future to know what will be. Being blinded to the potential results of our actions, we frequently do the wrong thing. In order to get along well in this world, you must learn to perceive accurately your immediate circumstances and surroundings, and to perceive also what you are headed for in the distant future.

—Paramahansa Yogananda,
in The Divine Romance

THE END OF THE WORLD

BY PARAMAHANSA YOGANANDA

Considering present world conditions, you can well appreciate why I have taken for my subject, "the end of the world." My talk today will help you to understand many things that are yet to come.

When we study current events, or those that have passed, our view of these happenings is determined by how clearly or distortedly they are reflected in our consciousness. People judge what happens according to the way they live, and by the measure of their own mind and intelligence. Self-interest, prejudices, hatred, and anger prevent true understanding of the events and mysteries of life. Only by communion with God can we comprehend His divine laws, which are working everywhere. In spite of all the ruthless, desecrating ways in which man has wrought destruction in

Extracts from a talk given at Self-Realization Fellowship Temple, Encinitas, California, May 26, 1940. The complete talk is published in The Divine Romance (Collected Talks and Essays, Volume II) *by Paramahansa Yogananda (Los Angeles: Self-Realization Fellowship).*

God's creation, still we will find that evil destroys itself, and that the power of God marches on in the face of every opposition.

The end of the world has various connotations, as I shall show you. First of all, there is the literal meaning. In this sense, the end of the world is of two kinds: partial dissolution and complete dissolution. It will be a long, long time before we can expect complete dissolution. Yet periodically some fanatical group predicts that the world is coming to an end. A few years ago we read in the papers about a sect in New York whose leader, misguided by mental phobia, or imagination, had frightened many of his followers by such a prediction. Those who seek to hold their followers by instilling fear in them are not true teachers. We should always be actuated by wisdom, never by fear.

To get back to my story: The members of this sect made ready for the coming holocaust. They gave their property away and went with their teacher to a mountaintop to await the end of the world. They waited and waited. Several days passed, and their hunger pangs were increasing. Still nothing happened, and they finally gave up. Eventually, they had to institute lawsuits in order to get back their property.

This is just one instance in which people have been alarmed by predictions of war or some other major disaster. More often than not, these proved to be false predictions. But in any case, we need not be frightened. After all, what is life? It is a temporary dream. Death is nothing but a sleep and another dream. When the dream is over, it is gone. . . . If you live for years in the mental world, whence God is sending forth these dreams of creation, and if you continuously work with the divine powers of the mind, you can see, as I do, all the mysteries of God's creation unfold before you.*

THE GOOD AND EVIL ACTIONS OF MAN AFFECT THE HARMÓNIOUS BALANCE OF THE EARTH

Partial dissolution of the world is brought on by the evil activities of people in general. If we all begin to fight with explosives, by this direct action we can reduce drastically the extent of civilization. And maybe if we work hard enough, we can dissolve this world, too! God has given man the power of destruction as well as the power of creation. We have made the world beautiful, and we have the power to destroy it. When we desecrate the world, the environment undergoes a violent change, which is called partial dissolution. Such upheavals have occurred many times — one example is Noah's flood. These partial dissolutions are due to the wrong actions and ignorant errors of mankind. Don't think the happenings of this world

---

* According to yoga philosophy, all creation originates in the creative thoughts of the Divine Mind, which manifest first as the causal or ideational universe, from which proceeds the astral universe of subtle energies and light, and finally the physical cosmos of material form.

are going on automatically without God's knowledge. And don't think that man's actions have no
effect on the operation of His cosmic laws. Everything that has happened throughout the ages is
recorded in the ether. The vibrations of evil that
mankind leaves in the ether upset the normal harmonious balance of the earth. When the earth becomes very heavy with disease and evil, these
etheric disturbances cause the world to give way
to earthquakes, floods, and other natural disasters.

It is the same as when you live wrongly for a
long time; various inharmonies begin to manifest
in your body, as well as certain diseases. Disease is
not a punishment. It is a poison that you yourself
create in the body, and the Lord wants you to get
rid of it. But all too often, by the time you try to
throw it off, the body has become completely de-
ranged, and you die. So, just like the human body,
the earth suffers from inharmonies and disease.
And it is because the combined actions of all people all over the world affect the planet on which
we live. There is no question about that. The good
and bad karmic conditions created by man determine and influence the climate; they affect the
wind and the ocean, even the very structure of the
earth, sometimes causing earthquakes.* All the ha-

* *Karma:* Effects of past actions, from this or previous lifetimes; from
the Sanskrit *kri,* to do. The equilibrating law of karma is that of action
and reaction, cause and effect, sowing and reaping. In the course of
natural righteousness, every human being by his thoughts and actions
becomes the molder of his own destiny. Whatever energies he himself,
wisely or unwisely, has set in motion must return to him as their start-

tred, the anger, the evil we send out into the world, and the agony and rebellion they cause — all these are disturbing the magnetic force of the earth, like static in the ether. In the destruction caused by this war we are seeing a partial dissolution of the world — dissolution of lives, money, homes.* In many ways it is worse than Noah's flood; it is a flood of fire and bloodshed. But one thing is encouraging: the good karma of mankind is greater than the evil karma. If this were not so, the earth would explode from the negative vibrations. Contrary to appearances, the earth is in an ascending cycle, and good will triumph.

THE LIFE CYCLES OF THE EARTH

The world is a sort of living being, with a predetermined age. We are the children of this great mother earth. We suckle her breast to partake of the food she produces. She also nurtures us through the circulating currents of oxygen, the sunshine, and the water of her atmosphere. Just as we go through youth, middle age, old age, death, and reincarnation, so also does the mother earth. There is the young mother earth, the middle-aged

---

ing point, like a circle inexorably completing itself. The cumulative actions of human beings within communities, nations, or the world as a whole constitute mass karma, which produces local or far-ranging effects according to the degree and preponderance of good or evil. The thoughts and actions of every person, therefore, contribute to the good or ill of this world and all peoples in it.

* This talk was given during World War II.

mother earth, and the old-aged mother earth. The
earth "dies" through partial dissolution, then rein-
carnates again to give human beings new life, new
strength, a new habitat in which to work out their
karma. Many times the earth has undergone partial
dissolution and reincarnation. But complete death

THE YUGAS, OR WORLD CYCLES

BY BROTHER ACHALANANDA

In *The Holy Science,* Swami Sri Yukteswar, Paramahansa Yogananda's guru, explains that human
civilization follows a definite cycle of evolution and
devolution, upward and downward through four
ages or *yugas.* In the scriptures of India these four
ages are called Kali Yuga (which lasts for 1,200
years), Dwapara Yuga (2,400 years), Treta Yuga
(3,600 years), and Satya Yuga (4,800 years). These
correspond to the less specific Greek concepts of
Iron Age, Bronze Age, Silver Age, and Golden Age.
Many illustrations from history could be given to
show the workings of these ascending and descending cycles, which consist of 12,000 years of
upward evolution of civilization followed by 12,000
years of gradual degeneration.

With the rise and fall of these cycles, man's ability to grasp the true nature of creation and of himself increases and decreases correspondingly. In
Kali Yuga, when man in general is completely

will come to the earth only when it dissolves back
again into God.

I will explain briefly about the life cycles of the
earth. These cycles consist of 24,000 years, divided
into four *yugas* or ages — 12,000 years of ascending
through these *yugas* to increasing enlightenment,

---

blinded by *maya* (cosmic delusion), he cannot conceive of anything subtler than the physical attributes of the world around him — solids, liquids,
gases. During this period man is totally absorbed in
the problems of material existence — food, shelter,
fuel for warmth, the other basic necessities for
physical survival. As the cycle ascends to Dwapara
Yuga, his consciousness becomes refined to the
point where he can go beyond gross outer forms
and comprehend the subtler forces — the atomic
and electromagnetic structure of creation. In Treta
Yuga he advances further, and gains knowledge and
power over the attributes of universal magnetism,
the underlying source of all electrical forces. And in
the highest age, Satya Yuga, his consciousness is at-
tuned to the presence of God — the creative power
emanating from the Divine, which sustains the universe through vibration. In the descending half of
the cycle, this process is reversed.

A more complete discussion of the *yugas* may
be found in *The Holy Science,* by Swami Sri Yukteswar (published by Self-Realization Fellowship).

and then 12,000 years of descending through the *yugas* to increasing ignorance and materialism. Each of these half-cycles is called a Daiva Yuga. The earth has already passed through many complete cycles since the dawn of creation. The four ages of each Daiva Yuga are Kali Yuga, the dark or materialistic age; Dwapara Yuga, the electrical or atomic age; Treta Yuga, the mental age; and Satya Yuga, the age of truth or enlightenment.

Dwapara Yuga, the Present Cycle

The earth has already passed through Kali Yuga, the materialistic age of 1,200 years' duration. According to the calculations of my guru, Swami Sri Yukteswar, we are about 240 years into Dwapara Yuga, the second age, which consists of 2,400 years. Now in its ascendancy, this is the electrical age, even though it may yet seem very materialistic. If you think about it, you will see how man has progressed from comprehending only gross matter to understanding and harnessing the energy in matter. In this age, man will make great headway in the electrical or electromagnetic field of science.

As Dwapara Yuga progresses, diseases will be treated and healed more and more by rays. Vibratory energy can reach the electronic factors of the atoms, the building blocks of matter, where gross chemicals cannot penetrate. After this war, you will see a great surge of development in electrical science. Aviation will develop tremendously also. Travel will be much, much more by air. Planes are still viewed with doubt by many today, just as trains were once looked upon with fear; but planes are already taking over, and trains have become almost a thing of the past. Gradually, automobiles will come to be considered as carts.

The trouble in this second age is that there is not enough security, because science plays the part of Dr. Jekyll and Mr. Hyde. Man uses science not only to create and do good, but to destroy as well. Therefore scientific development is not yet safe. The present World War shows how the technology of science is being used to destroy mankind. Out of the conflict we will learn how to employ more scientific devices for human comfort. But unless we develop spiritual forces, we will also continue to use scientific knowledge to destroy.

People will learn from this war the devastating consequences of the misuse of technology. In the First World War, and in earlier times, it was considered chivalrous to fight. But the idea of chivalry has gone. In this war, no one wants to fight. After it is over, there will be so much fear of world devastation that if anybody tries to start a war, the rest of the world will fall upon that nation. I am telling you things far ahead of my time....

Man's destructive potential has grown much greater than his constructive power. There will be no safety in the electrical age. Methods of war on a greater and greater scale will come. So thank

Paramahansa Yogananda's
predictions on....

How Our World Will Change

*From a magazine article published in April 1942,
in which Paramahansa Yogananda made the following predictions about how the world will
change as it moves into the new era:*

America and India, situated on opposite
sides of the earth, will represent the two highest types of ideal material civilization and ideal
spiritual civilization. They will influence the
whole world with their combined civilization.
The material efficiency of America combined
with the spiritual efficiency of India will lead
the world to a balanced existence.

Science and religion will join hands to prevent the misuse of science in wars and to free
religion from superstition, thus giving all the
world a securer civilization.

Experimental psychology will investigate
religious methods and yoga techniques for human perfection and God-contact.

No matter what happens, the world will become better and better until the United States
of India, of Asia, of Europe, and of the Ameri-
cas are achieved and become ready to amal-
gamate into the United States of the World.

The United States of the World will not
come in a day nor in our lifetime, but a great
deal of groundwork will be prepared in this
twentieth century.

God that Dwapara Yuga, the electrical age, is only 2,400 years.

TRETA YUGA

Next we will come to Treta Yuga, the third era or age, of 3,600 years' duration. That is the mental age, when most people will use mind power. The power of the mind will be much more highly developed than it is now. To a great extent, everything will be accomplished by that power. There will be an increase of wisdom, and therefore more safety in that age; people will make a stronger effort to use peaceful means for settling their problems. There will be less use of electricity, and growing use of the power of the mind. This is not to say that everyone will be able to know others' minds. But just as there are powerful radios that can tune in even weak stations, and weak radios that can pick up only strong stations, so some people will have stronger mental powers than others in the age of the mind.

In that mental age, by the power of the mind we will be able to know our fellow beings better, so that it will be difficult for anyone to be wicked. There will be very little hypocrisy, because people are hypocritical only when they think others do not know their real feelings. As a result of greater understanding, humanity will learn to live more peacefully with one another. Mind power will be used for healing and as food for the body.

Satya Yuga

After the third age will come Satya Yuga, or the age of truth, when the mind of man will be able to comprehend all mysteries of creation, and to live in communion with God. People of this age will find no barrier between the material world and the astral heaven — they will be able to enter the astral world and commune with those souls who have gone on to that sphere. The ascending Satya Yuga will last for 4,800 years. Many fully evolved souls will find liberation in that *yuga,* more than in any of the other ages.*

But even the end of Satya Yuga will not signal the end of the world. The cycle will be continuous, descending and reascending through all four ages again and again. Intermittently, cataclysms will occur, in which the world will die and then begin anew its continuous cycle. The earth was created to bring souls to their divine destiny; it is carrying a heavy burden. Until all our work is done — until our souls evolve back to God — this earth will never totally dissolve. It is only when God no longer needs it for the evolution of souls that the world will be no more. Then will come the real end of the world. So don't be afraid that our earth will tumble into the oven of the sun, which is so hot that all things would melt and va-

* "Most anthropologists, believing that 10,000 years ago humanity was living in a barbarous Stone Age, summarily dismiss as 'myths' the widespread traditions of very ancient civilizations in Lemuria, Atlantis, India, China, Japan, Egypt, Mexico, and many other lands." — *Autobiography of a Yogi*

porize in just a few seconds. The ultimate end of
the world is far off. It has a lot of work to do yet.

RISE ABOVE THE AGE IN
WHICH YOU ARE BORN

You do not have to wait for the end of the
world in order to be free. There is another way:
rise above the age in which you are born. In the
material age, the majority of mankind is materially
minded. But you will also find those who are living ahead of their times, Christlike souls. In the
mental and electrical ages, you will find predominant the mentalities characteristic of those *yugas*.
At the same time, there are other mentalities —
some that are more highly evolved, and others not
yet as highly evolved. Thus in this electrical age
you can find people who are still living in the
stone age. There is always a balance: some who
are living ahead and some who are living behind
the age of civilization in which they are born.

Through repeated incarnations, those of lesser
development will gradually advance until they express the mentality of the age in which they rein-
carnate, and eventually, the qualities characteristic
of the higher ages yet to come. The cycles of this
world are like a see-saw going up and down. But
when we hasten our evolution through right living
and a spiritual technique such as Kriya Yoga,* we

* An advanced technique of God-communion. See page 83.

live ahead of our time and can find freedom in God within this or only a few lifetimes.

Another way in which we experience the end of the world is in the detachment that is felt in sleep, in dreams, in losing one's mind, and in death. These conditions are forced on us; so it seems that the experience of the end of the world is necessary to us. Its purpose is to teach us the delusive nature of the world and the true nature of our Self, the soul. The soul comes on earth and becomes entangled in the mesh of delusion. Through the suffering that comes to us then, the Lord wants us to see that the world is not perfect. In this way He helps us to break our attachment to it. God is trying to make us realize, through nonidentification with it, how delusive our existence here is. The more I saw of the world and its defects, the greater became my determination to know God.

The World Ends for Us
in Divine Ecstasy

In a metaphysical sense, the end of all earthly desires is the end of the world. For your own happiness, you must strive to live free of worldly desires. If there is anything you can't do without, you still have a terrible lesson to learn. Imagine yourself taken away from this earth with all of your desires unfulfilled. They are like cankers in your soul. You would have to return here many times, enduring heartaches and disappointments again and again, to cure yourself of those desires.

It is far better to say to God, "Lord, I didn't ask You to create me. I am here because You put me here. I will do the best I can, but I have no desires except to do Your will. I don't want to be sent back here to suffer any more. I don't want to go on endlessly returning, sometimes as a rich man, sometimes as a poor man; sometimes with ill health and disease; sometimes with sorrows, sometimes with snatches of happiness. I am not a mortal being. I am the immortal soul."...

Live without being attached. Wherever you are, carry within your bosom a portable heaven of joy. Remember that you are here in this world to be entertained. When you go to a movie, whether you see a tragedy, or a comedy, or a drama, you say afterward, "Oh, it was a good movie!" So must you look upon life. Have no fear. If you live in fear, health will go. Rise above disease and troubles. While you try to remedy your condition, inwardly be untouched by it. Be strong inside, with full faith in God. Then you will conquer all the limitations of the world; you will be a king of peace and happiness. That is what I want you to be.

The Lord gives you that freedom every night, in sleep. When you retire, say to Him, "Lord, the world has ended for me. I am resting in Thine arms. Thou hast put me here to watch Thy movies of life: tragedy and laughter, health and disease, life and

death, wealth and poverty, war and peace — these
are naught but dreams to entertain me. Untouched,
I rest in the thought of Thee, the only Reality."

Last of all, the end of the world is realized in
samadhi, or divine ecstasy. There are two kinds of
samadhi. When at first you try to sit and meditate,
your mind runs away in all directions. You think it
is impossible to go deep. But if you sit still and
persist long enough, you will begin to feel that
wonderful silence of God. When your mind is
withdrawn, centered in Him, the world is forgotten and you find in that silence a happiness greater
than any worldly pleasure. That state, when you
are totally absorbed in inner awareness of God, no
longer conscious of the world, is called *sabikalpa
samadhi.* It is "partial dissolution of the world"
because, when you return to ordinary consciousness, the delusions of the world will again somewhat affect you, unless you are highly evolved and
free of all desires and attachments.

The second and highest state of *samadhi* is
when you are in the world but not of it — carrying
on your duties, but every moment conscious of
God. That is *nirbikalpa samadhi.* It is the end of
all limiting desires and attachments. Delusion is van-
quished, and that is the true end of the world....

End Your Dream Delusions in God

End the world for yourself now, by being with
God. Don't desecrate the temple of your soul with

restless desires and boisterous worldly pleasures. Stand immaculate in the light of your conscience, and in the light of love for God. Reach that stage now. Then, perhaps during war in this electrical age, or in the mental age, or in the truth age, you will come like a Christ to give peace on earth and to say to mankind: "I learned the lessons God wanted me to learn. Troubles, diseases, and death mean nothing to me. I am one with the Eternal Light. The world has ended for me. Come, my brothers and sisters who are still suffering from the nightmare of this world of life and death and endless rounds of incarnations — come with me! I will show you that the end of the world means the end of your dream delusions of this earth. Learn this lesson so that your soul may shine forever — an eternal star — in the bosom of the great Lord."

Remember, you are here on earth for only a little while, but you are God's child for eternity.

GUIDANCE AND ENCOURAGEMENT
FOR THE YEARS AHEAD

BY SRI DAYA MATA

A question I have often received, especially in recent years, is how to deal with the problems of the troubled times in which we are living. People from all parts of the world are concerned about the sad state of affairs affecting our planet.

Throughout history, the human race has gone through so many crises, and these predicaments will continue to come and go. This world revolves in an upward and downward cycle that continually repeats itself. Right now, the consciousness of society as a whole is progressing upward; after reaching its apex thousands of years hence, it will come down again. Progression, regression; there is constant ebb and flow on this plane of duality.

Compilation of talks printed in Self-Realization *magazine. Sri Daya Mata is Paramahansa Yogananda's spiritual successor as president of Self-Realization Fellowship/Yogoda Satsanga Society of India.*

With these evolutional cycles, civilizations rise and fall. Consider the highly advanced past civilizations, such as those of India and China. From the ancient Sanskrit epics of India, for example, we see that during the time of Sri Rama, thousands of years before the Christian era, technology was highly advanced, as evidenced by his marvelous aircraft. And greater still were the mental and spiritual powers of those who lived in that Golden Age. But eventually, civilization began to decline, until in the Dark Ages such advancement became obscured. What caused this? I was thinking about that yesterday after my meditation, in light of what is happening in the world today.

The Nature of the Present Crisis

During the downward part of the cycle, people in general become increasingly ignorant of the spiritual side of their nature, until all that is noble disappears. Then the fall of that civilization is not far behind. This same process can happen to nations in the ascending phase of the cycle as well. If man's moral and spiritual evolution does not keep pace with the upward progress of knowledge and technology, he misuses the power he has acquired, to his own destruction. Indeed, this is the nature of the world crisis we are facing today.

Man's consciousness has evolved enough for him to unlock the mystery and marvelous power of the atom, a power that may one day perform tremendous things that we cannot even dream about now. But what have we done with that knowledge? The primary concentration has been on the development of instruments of destruction. Modern technology has also given us freedom from many of the time-consuming tasks that were once necessary for physical survival. Often, however, the leisure time man has gained is not used to advance his mental and spiritual natures, but to engage in an endless pursuit of material and sensual pleasures. If man thinks only in terms of his own sensuality, ruled by his emotions of hatred, jealousy, lust, and greed, the inevitable result is inharmony between individuals, turmoil within societies, conflicts among nations. Wars have never cured anything; instead, they snowball into greater holocausts — one confrontation breeding another. Only by the evolution of wiser, more loving human beings will the world become a truly better place.

***

A PROMISE OF LIGHT

Someone asked me how we can best deal with the negation and darkness that are so prevalent in the world today. I prayed very deeply about that, and my mind went back to the divine experience that I had in India thirty years ago during a pilgrimage to Mahavatar Babaji's cave.*

* Sri Daya Mata recounts the story of this pilgrimage in her book, *Only Love,* in the chapter entitled, "A Blessing From Mahavatar Babaji." It was

My companions and I were spending the night in a little hut on the way to the cave. In the middle of the night, I had a superconscious vision in which I saw that the world was going to face a very difficult time, a period of great turmoil and unrest and confusion. I cried out, and the others asked me what was wrong. I didn't want to talk about the experience then; but I knew it had deep meaning, not merely for Daya Ma but for the world. In this vision there was a huge dark cloud spreading out over the universe; its ominous darkness was horrifying to see. But in the next instant, I saw the great, divinely loving, all-blissful light of God pushing back the black waves of that cloud. And I knew then that all would eventually turn out well.

We are now passing through the troubled times foretold in that experience. It is happening in every nation — wars, famine, incurable diseases, economic crises, catastrophic disasters, religious and civil strife. Worst of all, there is a growing sense of fear and helplessness in the face of advancing chaos.

Why are these afflictions upon us? Our situation is not unlike that of the ancient Egyptians, who were stricken by plagues and calamities for having defied the Divine Will, as is recorded in the scriptures. We tend to think that such occurrences happened only in biblical times, but this is not so. We have plagues

---

Mahavatar Babaji who in 1861 restored to the world the spiritual science of Kriya Yoga, which had been lost for centuries. (See page 90 n.) More information about his life and spiritual mission is given in *Autobiography of a Yogi. (Publisher's Note)*

today, many of them. We blindly think, "Oh, these can't be the result of our having transgressed. It's just a coincidence." It is not a coincidence.

Laws of Right Behavior Are Part of the Universal Order

Ask yourselves: "How far have we wandered from truth?" "Thou shalt not kill; thou shalt not commit adultery; thou shalt not steal...." These laws of truth have been expounded in the Ten Commandments, in the teachings of Christ, and, much earlier, in the Eightfold Path of Yoga — the first two steps of Patanjali's Yoga are *yama* and *niyama,* the principles of right behavior we should embrace and the principles of wrong behavior we should shun.*

These are divine laws, a part of the universal absolutes, which have been set before mankind by our beloved God. He created this world in the most scientific and mathematically precise manner; every aspect of it is governed by law. He makes His laws clear to us through revelation to great souls such as Jesus and the *rishis* of ancient India. He put forth these laws that we might have guidelines to help us learn how to behave in order to put our lives in tune with God.

Down through the ages have come great lovers of God with their divine messages. In early times

---

* Patanjali was the foremost ancient exponent of yoga. His date is uncertain, though many scholars assign him to the second century B.C. His Eightfold Path of Yoga is described on pages 159–60.

we had the principles expounded by Moses; for example, "An eye for an eye, a tooth for a tooth." He pointed out the inexorability of the divine law that what you sow, you must reap. Centuries later came Jesus Christ, bringing a teaching of great compassion. At that time humanity needed to learn something of forgiveness and mercy; there had been too many years of vengeance in "an eye for an eye, a tooth for a tooth." Christ sought to balance the exacting, uncompromising emphasis on law by teaching forgiveness, sharing, divine love. His influence has continued down to the present time.

Now we have entered another era — a time, Paramahansaji* has told us, when Mahavatar Babaji in communion with Jesus Christ has sent that which will enable humanity to go beyond merely hearing and talking about the teachings of Christ, or merely reading or reciting from India's great scripture, the Bhagavad Gita, for mankind is hungering for something deeper.

That "something" is direct communion with the Divine Beloved. Not one of us is outside of that Divine Awareness. We are all made in His image. Regardless of our color, our creed, our beliefs, we are all a part of Him; each one of us has within us that spark of the Divine. Scripture tells us: "Know ye not that ye are the temple of God, and that the Spirit of God dwelleth in you?"†

---

* *Ji* is a respectful suffix added to Indian names.

† I Corinthians 3:16. Cf. "I have said, Ye are gods; and all of you are children of the most High" (Psalms 82:6).

What is that spirit of God within us? It is the soul, the *atman;* the very essence of what we are. But how many of us know ourselves as divine souls? Most people have wandered so far away from that realization that they have no remembrance of the Divine for even one minute out of the day. Their consciousness has become jaded through abuse of the senses. The sense of taste has become jaded by alcohol, greed, wrong eating habits. The eyes have become jaded by the sensuality we behold in our daily lives. The ears have become jaded by all of the evil things we hear. And tongues have become jaded because they spew foul words reflecting dark thoughts.

***

WE ARE THE CREATORS OF WORLD CONDITIONS

We are the creators of the conditions that confront us. They are the sum total of immoral behavior and the decline of ethical standards in all walks of life.

The survival of civilization depends on observance of standards of right behavior. I am not talking about manmade codes that change with changing times, but about timeless universal principles of conduct that promote healthy, happy, peaceful individuals and societies — allowing for diversity in a harmonious unity.

It is sometimes hard for us in our ordinary consciousness to grasp the immensity of the truths behind God's structured universe. But those ultimate verities do exist, and there can be no compromise with the exacting laws by which the Lord upholds the cosmos and its beings. Everything in the universe is connected. As human beings, we are related not only to each other, but to all nature as well, because all life comes from one Source: God. He is perfect harmony; but the wrong thoughts and actions of man have a desultory effect on the manifestation of His harmonious plan in this world. Just as when you try to tune in a radio station, static may prevent you from receiving the program clearly, so man's "static" misbehavior disturbs the harmony of the forces of nature. Wars, natural catastrophes, social turmoil, and the other problems we are facing today are the result.

* * *

"Filled With God's Light and Joy"

We must change. That was the message of Paramahansa Yogananda; that is why this work he founded will grow on and on and on — because it can and will help people to change.

Afflicted by suffering, people commonly say: "Why did God do this to me?" He didn't do it to us. We must take responsibility for ourselves, for our own actions. When we hit a stone wall, the wall doesn't mean to hurt us; but we may break our knuckles, or our head! We cannot blame the wall for that.

We may lament, "But I didn't know that wall was there; otherwise I wouldn't have run into it!" That is why God created divine laws and set them forth as guidelines in all the great religions of the world. To each of us He is saying, "My child, these are the absolutes you must follow." He knew that we were weak; He knew that we were frail. He knew we had lost contact with Him — and that our vision and discrimination had been clouded — by our becoming too much immersed in this material world. So he gave those laws through the prophets and *rishis* to help us know when we are doing wrong. We suffer when we transgress those eternal divine principles.

We must get back to them. We must realize, as Christ said, that our kingdom is not of this world. It is beyond this mundane kingdom — it is where the divine ones are, where the great saints and masters are. How many times I saw Paramahansaji in his room suddenly become very quiet and withdrawn. Some of us were privileged on those occasions to sit at his feet and meditate with him. After he had opened his eyes, he would speak of that other world: "You see this finite world? It is so imperfect. If you could only see, as I see, that great world beyond this one — filled with God's light and joy."

My dear ones, your kingdom, too, is not of this world. Let us not lose our awareness of our real kingdom; let us not spend all of our time and attention on the things of this world, because one day we must leave it.

Do Not Accept "Doom and Gloom"

So when you ask me: "How do we face the 'doom and gloom' in this world?" I say to you: Don't

---

*Paramahansa Yogananda's
predictions on...*

Should we expect war and natural cataclysms?

From a lecture on March 6, 1938:

The sudden cataclysms that occur in nature, creating havoc and mass injury, are not "acts of God." Such disasters result from the thoughts and actions of man. Whenever the world's vibratory balance of good and evil is disturbed by an accumulation of harmful vibrations, the result of man's wrong thinking and wrong doing, you will see devastation....

The world will continue to have warfare and natural calamities until all people correct their wrong thoughts and behavior. Wars are brought about not by fateful divine action but by widespread material selfishness. Banish selfishness — individual, industrial, political, national — and you will have no more wars.

accept it! It doesn't exist as such unless you allow it to exist as darkness in your own consciousness. Make the effort to change the center of your awareness. How often each day do we think of God? How often do we turn inward to God? It is so wonderful to live always in the consciousness of His presence, to live always with the thought, "I love You, my God." What a thrill that is. "I love You, and because

---

When materiality predominates in man's consciousness, there is an emission of subtle negative rays; their cumulative power disturbs the electrical balance of nature, and that is when earthquakes, floods, and other disasters happen. God is not responsible for them! Man's thoughts have to be controlled before nature can be controlled.

Rama, an avatar who was one of India's great Hindu emperors, reigned over the kingdom of Ayodhya, whose inhabitants all lived righteously. It is said that during the golden era of Rama's rule no accidents or premature deaths or natural disasters disturbed Ayodhya's perfect harmony. There will be more harmony and health in every home as the individual members of the family live more rightly. When family members selfishly take away from one another, the house naturally will be filled with disharmony. So also with the nations; only when mankind lives rightly will the kingdom of God come on earth.

I love You first, I feel love for all mankind. I can forgive those who misunderstand me because I love You. I want only to do good in this world because I love You." That is the way we ought to live our lives.

Don't be discouraged by this "doom and gloom"; it will pass. In this world many civilizations have come and gone. There have been unnumbered crises like those we see today — more than we could possibly know or remember, though our souls have traveled through many such periods during our long journey of incarnations. But this is not all there is. There is something better for us beyond, in that other world. The more we take our minds away from the body's attachments to this sphere, the more we can lift our consciousness into that divine kingdom.

We begin by trying to spiritualize the senses. Look only to the good, try to think only good. It doesn't mean we become Pollyannas; it means we have the will, strength, devotion, and faith within us to say: "My God, I am Yours. And I will do whatever I can in my little corner of the world to cheer and uplift others — whether it be my family, my neighbors, my community, whomever I can reach. I will do the best I can, even though I myself may be struggling."

Our Guru* often said: "Real saints are those who, even in the midst of their own sufferings, bring cheer and healing into the lives of all who

* Reference to Paramahansa Yogananda. See footnote on page xi.

come to them." That is the attitude of a true lover of God. No matter what he or she is going through, no one who comes to that individual will go away feeling downtrodden, discouraged, a failure. We are all God's children; and we have, each one of us, that power by which we can conquer life's difficulties. But we must believe in it, we must exercise it — and we must strive always to be cheerful.

"A saint that is sad," Paramahansaji quoted, "is a sad saint!" He himself was most joyous, all the time — even in the midst of the tremendous struggles he went through to build this work of Self-Realization Fellowship/Yogoda Satsanga Society. To serve God isn't easy; in this world, *life* isn't easy! But let us live with joy, with cheerfulness, and with the determination that we *will* conquer, we *will* be all right, because the Divine is behind us.

Don't ever be a moody person; don't ever be one who spreads negative thinking. Remember: This world is created through the law of duality; there are two sides to everything — a positive and a negative — and each human being has the choice to align his consciousness with one or the other. No one wants to be around a stinkweed. It is negative and depresses us. But, as our Guru used to say, everybody loves to gather around a rose, which gives off a sweet fragrance. Be a positive human rose.

Make up your mind to be positive, to be cheerful, to be joyous. I promise you that if you do that, you will find good coming your way, because thought has the power to attract. If our thoughts

are habitually negative, we attract negative circumstances. If we live and think positively, we attract positive results. It's as simple as that: Like at-
tracts like.

***

THE POWER OF PRAYER TO
CHANGE THE WORLD

At the end of that vision I described, the darkness threatening our world was pushed away by
the spirit of God through increasing numbers of
individuals living according to spiritual principles.
Spirituality starts with morality, the rules of right
behavior that are basic to every religion — such as
truthfulness, self-control, faithfulness to marriage
vows, noninjury to others. And we must straighten
out not only our behavior, but also our thinking. If
we persist in thinking a certain way, those
thoughts eventually become actions. So to change
ourselves we have to begin with our thoughts.

Thought is a force; it has immense power. That
is why I believe so deeply in the Worldwide Prayer
Circle that Paramahansa Yogananda began. I hope
you are all involved in it. When people send forth
concentrated, positive thoughts of peace, love,
goodwill, forgiveness, as in the healing technique
used by the Worldwide Prayer Circle, this gener-
ates a great power. If the masses were to do this,
it would set up a vibration of goodness that would
be powerful enough to change the world.

CHANGE YOURSELF AND YOU WILL CHANGE THOUSANDS

Our role is to do everything we can to put our lives in attunement with God, that by our thoughts, our words, and our exemplary behavior we may reach out and exert some spiritual influence on the rest of the world. One's words have little meaning unless they are manifested in one's life. The words of Christ are as powerful today as they were two thousand years ago because he lived what he taught. Our lives also must quietly but eloquently reflect those principles we believe in. As our Guru often quoted, "Reform yourself and you will have reformed thousands."

You may say, "But there is so much in the world that needs correcting; so much to be done." Yes, the needs are formidable; but the world's troubles will not go away merely by our trying to correct the outer things. We have to correct the human element that is the real cause of these troubles, and we must begin with ourselves.

You can tell a person a thousand times not to smoke, but if he has made up his mind that he likes cigarettes, nothing you say is going to change his habit. Only when he begins to cough and suffer the negative effects of smoking does it hit home and he realizes, "This is affecting *me;* now it's becoming something *I* have to think about." Similarly, your words alone may have little power to influence an inharmonious person to be more peaceful. But if that person senses a spirit of harmony and well-being flowing from your own peaceful nature, that is something tangible; it will have a beneficial effect on him.

ESTABLISH AN INNER HARMONY WITH YOUR SOUL AND WITH GOD

The peace and harmony so urgently sought by all cannot be had from material things or any outer experience; it is just not possible. Perhaps by watching a beautiful sunset or going to the mountains or seaside you might feel a temporary serenity. But even the most inspiring setting will not give you peace if you are inharmonious in your own being.

The secret of bringing harmony into the outer circumstances of your life is to establish an inner harmony with your soul and with God....

As more of mankind strives for that state, the crises that threaten our world will diminish. But we have to realize that this earth will never be perfect, because this is not our permanent home; it is a school, and its students are in different grades of learning. We have come here to go through all of life's experiences, good and sorrowful, and thereby to learn from them.

God is eternal, and so are we. His universe will go on and on in its ups and downs. It is for us to put ourselves in harmony with His laws of creation. Those who do so continue to evolve upward regardless of their outer circumstances or of the particular world cycle they are born in; and by the refinement of their consciousness, they find freedom in God.

In the ultimate sense, the salvation of each one of us rests totally with ourselves — how we face life; how we behave; whether we conduct our lives with honesty, sincerity, regard for others, and above all, with courage, faith, trust in God. It becomes simple if we concentrate on love for God. We will then want to do good, and to be good, because we find peace and wisdom and joy pouring into our consciousness from that One whence we have come.

How often Paramahansaji had us affirm with him that our lives are to be lived in the joy that is God:

From Joy I have come. In Joy I live, move, and have my being. And in that sacred Joy I will melt again.

Hold on to this truth, and you will see how that Joy inwardly sustains you no matter what comes into your life. That Joy becomes more real to you than the ever-changing events of this kaleidoscopic world.

Are We Really Entering
a Better Age?

By Brother Anandamoy

When we look at the world today, with all its problems, all the confusion and ignorance, it is hard to believe that we have entered a higher age. Nevertheless, we really have left behind the period of grossest materialism, Kali Yuga, and are quite far into the beginnings of Dwapara Yuga, the next stage in the ascending cycle. As we move into this atomic age, more and more of the finer forces of nature that were unknown in the Dark Ages are beginning to be harnessed, giving rise to global telecommunications, computers, advances in medicine, agriculture, transportation — all those technologies that are so radically changing the fabric of daily life. However, the Kali Yuga from which we have just emerged is still a very strong influence. Because of this, our culture

In this article, based on a talk given at a Self-Realization Fellowship Convocation in Los Angeles, Brother Anandamoy offers counsel and encouragement for dealing with the challenges of a world in transition.

tends still to use scientific advances not only to do good, but also to cater to our grosser materialistic instincts of selfishness, destruction, greed.

WHY THESE TIMES ARE SO TURBULENT

The influence of Kali Yuga will be left behind as the years go by. But during this period of transition there is great conflict between the tenacious Kali Yuga mindset and the more enlightened spiritual understanding struggling to be born. This is why our times are so turbulent. Even though it is true that we have entered a higher age, most people — in action, in understanding, in attitudes — are still very much in the Kali Yuga. The focus of their concentration is outward, on body satisfaction, ego satisfaction.

In this ascending age, with its modern technology, one of the greatest advantages is free time. Think of it: In the dark ages, people had to use every waking moment and all of their energy just to survive, just to make a living. Only a very, very few of the privileged classes had time to spend in higher pursuits. Now, at least in the industrialized countries, nearly everybody is in that class. But what do most people do with this luxury? Because of their nonunderstanding of what life is all about, they waste their time and dissipate their energy in endless diversions. The average American watches television forty-four hours a week. Can you imagine what could be done if that amount of time were invested in spiritual pursuits — how much more happy and fulfilled those people would be, and what a better world we would have? Those who meditate are putting that extra time to good use; but unfortunately, most of humanity has turned away from God and God's laws. That is why we have this tremendous mess in the world!

We think it would be wonderful if only we lived in peaceful, normal times. But in a way there is an advantage to living in troubled times — they impress on us more clearly that this world is not our home, that true security lies not in this outer world, and that we need to seek God. Consider those peaceful times when there was no fear of world war, when there was no problem with unemployment or ecology. It was during such an era in the last century that Thoreau observed: "The mass of men lead lives of quiet desperation." Why? Because still there was a hunger, a yearning; something essential was missing: God.

It is important to understand that wherever the world is in its upward and downward cycles, whatever stage of material or spiritual advancement exists outwardly, each soul progresses according to his or her individual efforts. Even in the darkest periods, in the worst conditions, there were men and women — perhaps not many, but there were some — who attained divine realization. That is why I urge you all not to pay too much attention to the times we are living in, but to focus on that which is essential — your spiritual efforts.

Concentrate on God, not on the outer show. Think of it: How many lives are behind us, and in those lives how many experiences have we had? Countless! Each of us has spent many lives as men, many as women. We have belonged to all different races and nationalities. We have been rich and poor, famous and forgotten. We have lived in times of peace and in times of war. Where are all those lives now? In themselves they had no value, other than in what we became spiritually through those experiences. Each of those lives presented opportunities to seek God and to grow. Obviously we didn't take full advantage of them — that is why we are still here! Why did we miss those opportunities? Because we concentrated so much on the external show and our external role that we pushed God out of our consciousness.*

LIVE IN THE PRESENT, AND FILL THAT PRESENT WITH GOD

Living in these times, of course we wonder about the future: "Will there be peace or war, prosperity or lack? What is going to happen?" This is natural. Still, we have to be careful, because if we are dwelling too much on these things, permitting speculation and worries to occupy our mind, God

* The doctrine of reincarnation, set forth in the scriptures of India, is that human beings, compelled by the law of evolution, incarnate repeatedly in progressively higher lives — retarded by wrong actions and desires, and advanced by spiritual endeavors — until Self-realization and God-union are attained.

again is pushed out. And then another incarnation — another opportunity to find Him who is the whole goal of life, the solution to all our problems — is wasted.

Many persons want a detailed preview of what's going to happen in the future. Why? So they can worry about it? This is exactly what the divine ones and the scriptures warn us against. Jesus said, "Sufficient unto the day is the evil thereof." Paramahansa Yogananda told us: "If we could but realize the effect on ourselves of the burdens we often place upon the mind, we might wonder that we have not had a breakdown long ago. Taxing our minds with all kinds of worries and anxieties, we are soon overwhelmed by the load. Fear creeps in as a result and we lose our mental poise and spiritual balance. The trouble with us is that instead of living only in the present, we try to live in the past and in the future at the same time. These loads are too heavy for the mind to carry."

Analyze your thoughts; usually you are escaping into the past or into the future. It is a total waste! Live in the present, and fill that present with God.

Now, I am not a fortune teller, so instead of giving you predictions about what is coming, I have a thought for you from Paramahansaji. He said: "When you see a motion picture or a stage performance, if you know the plot beforehand it will not be so interesting. It is good that you don't understand this life, because God is playing a movie drama in your life. It wouldn't be interesting if we

knew what was going to take place before it happened. Don't be anxious about what is to be in the
end. But always pray to God, 'Teach me to play my
part in this drama of life — weak or strong, sick or
well, high or low, rich or poor — with an immortal
attitude, that at the end of this drama I may know
the moral of it all.'"

AFFIRM YOUR DIVINE NATURE

In a previous talk I suggested to you all to write
on a piece of paper, "I am an immortal," and paste it
on the mirror of your bathroom, so that you see it
every morning and evening and carry that thought
throughout the day. Have you taken that sign off
your mirror? If so, put it back up! Remember what
you truly are. You are playing a role in the big drama
of creation, but you are not that role — you are an
immortal soul, made in the image of God.

"God's dream creation was not meant to
frighten you," Paramahansaji told us, "but to prod
you to realize finally that it has no reality. So why
be afraid of anything? Jesus said: 'Is it not written
in your law, I said, Ye are gods?'"

Many people have asked me: "Should we move
out to the country to be safe if anything should
happen?" Well, my dears, we cannot be so naive as
to think that the law of karma works only in the
cities! Out in the country a person can have a crip-
pling or a deadly accident, or cancer or something
else. When people asked the Master [Paramahansa

Yogananda] about cancer he said, "Certainly a cure for cancer will be found." But he went on: "However, don't think that the law of karma will stop working then. New diseases will come." So we have to cease thinking in terms of external conditions so much, and realize that there is no security anywhere, in anything, except in righteous living, in prayer and meditation, in attunement with God.

That is why Paramahansa Yogananda urged us: "Make a supreme effort to get to God. I am speaking practical truth to you, practical sense; and giving you a philosophy that will take away all of your consciousness of hurt. Be afraid of nothing. If death comes, all right. What is going to happen, will happen. Refuse to be intimidated by this dream. Affirm: 'I will not be frightened by ill health, poverty, and accidents. Bless me, O Lord, that when You put me through trials, I realize their delusive nature and become victorious over them by positive action and by remaining inwardly united to You.'...

"Don't be attached to the passing dreams of life. Live for God and God alone. This is the only way to have freedom and safety in this world. Outside of God there is no security; no matter where you go, delusion can attack you. Be free right now. Be a son of God now; realize you are His child, so that you may be rid of this dream of delusion forever. Meditate deeply and faithfully, and one day you will wake up in ecstasy with God and see how foolish it is that people think they are suffering. You and I and they are all pure Spirit."

Perfection, ultimate fulfillment, is not meant to be found in this world. I am not giving you a negative picture of life, but pointing out, as Jesus said, our kingdom is not of this world. This is not the kingdom of God. It is not our home; we don't belong here permanently. This is only school. When we forget why we are here. that is when our troubles begin.

"ALL IS LIGHT, ALL IS JOY, ALL IS PEACE, ALL IS LOVE"

When people come to me for personal counsel, in about eight cases out of ten I give them the following passage from *Man's Eternal Quest.** These are strong words, but they give the whole truth about life in a nutshell:

"There is nothing to live for except God. All else will go. Pray only for That which is abiding. Don't yearn for human love; it will vanish. Behind human love is the spiritual love of God. Seek that. Don't pray for home or for money or for love or for friendship. Don't pray for anything of this world. Enjoy only what the Lord gives to you. All else leads to delusion.

"Man has come on earth solely to learn to know God; he is here for no other reason. This is the true message of the Lord. To all those who

* Volume I of Paramahansa Yogananda's collected talks and essays, published by Self-Realization Fellowship.

seek and love Him, He tells of that great Life where there is no pain, no old age, no war, no death — only eternal assurance. In that Life nothing is destroyed. There is only ineffable happiness that will never grow stale — a happiness always new.

"So that is why it is worthwhile to seek God. All those who sincerely seek Him will surely find Him. Those who want to love the Lord and yearn to enter His kingdom, and who sincerely wish in their hearts to know Him, will find Him. You must have an ever-increasing desire for Him, day and night. He will acknowledge your love by fulfilling His promise to you throughout eternity, and you shall know joy and happiness unending. All is light, all is joy, all is peace, all is love. He is all."

Now, he is not talking against human friendship or marriage, or seeking outward success. These are part of our earthly schooling. He is speaking about discrimination: to renounce, once and for all, the thought that anything, any condition, in this world can give us happiness.

That consciousness does not make life dark or negative. Look at the saints; they are the happiest of people, because they are centered in God while playing their external role with full enthusiasm. Even when outwardly they are going through difficult, even horrible, experiences, that inner joy remains.

For instance, consider Saint Thérèse of Lisieux, the "Little Flower," who died of tuberculosis when she was twenty-five. It was a terrible disease, a slow suffocation as the lungs were destroyed; and at the same time she was starving because the disease had also devastated her digestive system so she could not assimilate food anymore. One time her older sister, who lived in the same convent, was visiting her in the infirmary; she began crying at the suffering Thérèse was going through.

"Why are you crying?" Thérèse asked.

"Because you are suffering so much!" the sister replied.

"Yes," little Thérèse said. "But peace, too. Peace!"

Even then she was centered in God. This is what we too can, and must, learn.

There Is a Reality That Is Immortal and Eternal

Practice yoga, the techniques of meditation. Lord Krishna in the Bhagavad Gita (V:6) says: "Without yoga, O Arjuna, renunciation (of material consciousness) is difficult to achieve. By the practice of yoga, the *muni* ('he whose mind is absorbed in God') quickly attains the Infinite." If we are not practicing meditation, we remain in outer consciousness, body-identified, identified totally with our external experiences and the external show. Through yoga, we interiorize our consciousness, gradually experiencing more and more the Reality behind this passing show.

The more you bring God into your life, the more you can say what Brother Lawrence, a beautifully humble and devotional saint of the seventeenth century, said: "I do not know what God has in store for me. I am in such tranquility that I fear nothing. What could I fear when I am with Him? I stay there as much as I can. May He be blessed for everything."

Isn't that wonderful? That is truth. That is security. There is a Reality that is immortal and eternal, that is not touched by anything this world is going through. Don't concentrate on the external show. Concentrate on God.

"Live today well, and the next step will take care of itself," Paramahansa Yogananda said. "Events proceed according to a beautiful divine plan." What is that plan? That all of us reach the end of our journey, our immortal home of bliss. The Master tells us: "Trust fully in God. He never fails you. Ever cling to Him, for behind the shadows you are in His immortal arms."

Be Nourished by the Soul

The Art of Balanced Spiritual Living

By Sri Daya Mata

In the last decades of this present millennium, we have seen the world change so rapidly — our way of life literally transformed in the space between one generation and the next. Where is it all leading? Our guru, Paramahansa Yogananda, impressed on us the understanding that whenever world conditions or civilizations undergo significant changes, there is always an underlying subtle cause — the hidden working of the law of karma that operates in the lives of individuals and on a mass level of international affairs. Just as with challenges in our personal life the right attitude is, "What am I to learn from this?" so the world as a whole needs to understand the lessons that the Divine intends us to assimilate at this point in our evolution.

Humankind has to embrace the art of balanced spiritual living, and it has to learn to get along as one global family. The pressures we feel and the anxieties that plague us in this era of exploding technological advances will sooner or later compel us to learn these lessons. Paramahansaji foresaw this years ago, and told us many times: "The day is coming when the world will have to get back to simple living. We must simplify our lives to make time for God. We must live more with the consciousness of brotherhood, because as civilization evolves into a higher age, we are going to find that the world becomes smaller. Prejudice, intolerance, must go."

Jesus said, "A house divided against itself cannot stand." Science has brought the nations so close to one another that the once vast world is now more like a household, with each member interlinked and dependent on the others. Considering how difficult it is for even a small family to stay together amidst the disuniting trends of our times, is there hope for unity in the world at large? There *is* hope — for individual families as well as for relationships among the global family of nations — if we make time to nurture those goals and values that are conducive to real peace and spiritual understanding.

Attributes of a Balanced Life

Humanity today is suffering from spiritual malnutrition. People in parts of the world are suffering from physical starvation, but millions in all nations are suffering from spiritual starvation. Science has given the means to feed every person on this planet; it is man's spiritual poverty that makes him cling to selfishness and small-minded prejudices, thereby preventing him from eradicating hunger and other forms of deprivation.

As Paramahansaji often said: "America and other countries in the West are the most prosperous starving nations in the world." We do not adequately nourish the qualities of the soul. With all of the material gain we have achieved, millions in the most advanced nations are discontented, unhappy, bewildered as to the meaning of their existence. But see the Divine Hand in this: the Lord has set up this cosmic schoolhouse in such a way as to ensure our upward evolution. If we were contented, there would be no impetus for progress; dissatisfaction motivates us to improve situations. So it is that the stresses and pressures of our modern life are pointing the way to the next step in our development.

We are more and more realizing, particularly in the Western world, that the goals we have pursued do not satisfy our souls. Over the next generation or so, we will see this same understanding emerge in those developing nations where Western materialistic values are being overly idolized and imitated. We have accomplished much in improving the outer conditions of life, but we have neglected the most important accomplishment — to improve and change ourselves, to know ourselves, to understand why we are born, to realize our true purpose in life.

"The goal of life is to know truth," Paramahansaji said. "We may think we have other goals, and we may have lesser goals; but eventually, in one life or in another, man comes to the realization that he has but one goal to achieve, and that is to know himself in truth as the soul, the *atman,* made in the image of God; and to know Him who is Truth: God."

When we speak of spiritual poverty, remember: it is not our souls that are starved. The soul is infinite, inexhaustible bliss, life, love that sustain every faculty of our being. It is when we shut ourselves off from the soul that our peace, understanding, kindness, courage, compassion — all the noble qualities of the spirit — remain undernourished, undeveloped, in some people seemingly nonexistent! The divine manna of the soul is not something we have to acquire. We have it already and do not know it. We have only to learn, as the scripture tells us, "Be still, and know that I am God." Be still, and into your consciousness flows the realization that you are an immortally blissful ray of the Divine Spirit, an eternal being of infinite wisdom and infinite love, residing for a time in this little bodily temple. That is the truth of our being, but who lives in that consciousness? Who nurtures the expression of that wondrous being?

The life anchored in truth, in wisdom, in God, is a balanced life. It starts with meditation. That is the emphasis of the routine established by Paramahansa Yogananda for those of us who reside in his ashrams. The way of life he taught us consists of meditation first thing in the morning, before we begin our daily duties, and at intervals throughout the day: at noon, and again in the early evening when we have finished our daily work, and once more late at night alone in our rooms before retiring.*

You might say, "Well, that is all right for those who live in an ashram. It is not possible for me; I have too many other responsibilities!" If you think that way, you have written your own verdict, because no one can have a balanced life who does not make time for God. This is a valuable lesson the Divine intends that humanity learn as the world advances into a higher age. Technology has so accelerated the pace of life — getting and doing and having, faster, faster, faster! — that most people take little or no time to realize those goals and values that bring balance and peace. It is impossible to be balanced human beings and forget God, because His very essence in us is all we really want or need. To forget Him is to deny our real Self, our inmost nature, and to invite inharmony and lack of success in all departments of our life.

It is the spiritually balanced individual who is truly successful. I am not referring to monetary success; it has little meaning. That has been my experience, as it was Paramahansaji's: I have met scores of materially successful human beings who

* Paramahansa Yogananda taught that dawn, noon, sunset, and midnight correspond with the four seasons: dawn with spring, noon with summer, sunset with fall, and midnight with winter. The daily "seasons" cause bodily changes. Science, too, has documented that the human body goes through measurable cycles throughout the day, proving that man does indeed react to an inner and an outer cosmic clock. Practice of meditation during these changing cycles of the day brings definite revitalizing effects, physically, mentally, and spiritually.

have been emotional and spiritual failures — stressful; lacking inner peace and the ability to give and receive love; unable to relate harmoniously to their families, or to other human beings, or to God. A person's success cannot be measured by what he has, only by what he is and what he is able to give of himself to others.

Meditation helps us to align our outer life with the inner values of the soul as nothing else in this world can. It does not take away from family life or relationships with others. On the contrary, it makes us more loving, more understanding — it makes us want to serve our husband, our wife, our children, our neighbors. Real spirituality begins when we include others in our wish for well-being, when we expand our thoughts beyond "I and me and mine."

Reexamine Your Priorities

Decades ago our Guru spoke in these terms to thousands. Many took his counsel to heart; but for the masses he was perhaps a bit ahead of his time! He once observed: "When Hindu teachers say, 'Meditate, and cultivate inner peace and happiness,' modern man says, 'That is old-fashioned. Those unprogressive Hindus! What do they know of our wonderful civilization: our excellent sanitation system, our big comfortable cars, our beautiful dresses we change every year according to the fashions, our fine homes?' And the Hindu will say,

'Yes, but what about your wonderful bills and taxes? And what about your fast-paced life, which gives you no peace of mind? All these "wonderful" things have made you slave-drivers of yourselves. You are nothing but nervous wrecks. The only little pleasure you have is in thinking that in having more money you will have more happiness.' But after people get it, they want more still."

Fifty years later, world changes are compelling people to reexamine their priorities — to realize that without a rebirth of spiritual values this modern era will grow ever more chaotic, insecure, and inharmonious. But while there may be less indifference to spirituality and meditation today than during our Guru's life, instead there now is a sense of helplessness: "I don't have time!" Those who are able to schedule endless activities throughout the day, but not a few minutes to be with God, need to reevaluate their busyness. Their real problem is not a lack of time, but an addiction to restlessness; and it is going to take more than simply using a new type of weekly planning calendar to cure it.

Addiction is a disease; and addiction to restlessness is an epidemic spiritual disease. Paramahansaji spoke of it this way: "Spiritual disease manifests itself in lack of soul peace, want of poise, discontentment, restlessness, unbalance, inharmony, unkindness, unwillingness to meditate, and the habit of putting off meditation." Until people acknowledge that we are dealing not with a sched-

uling conflict but with a spiritual sickness that requires a specific cure, their efforts to live a spiritually balanced life will remain mostly on the level
of vague, ineffectual intentions.

The drug addict feels an intense craving for the
addictive substance. As long as he indulges that
craving, his enslavement simply gets worse. Is it
not the same with the modern restlessness addiction? People feel empty within because of their unbalanced concentration on temporary satisfaction
supplied by material acquisitions. They are trying
desperately to assuage that empty restlessness by
indulging in more restlessness! They occupy themselves with useless diversions to distract the mind
from problems just enough to somehow get
through each day: "Well, if I can go shopping in
the mall, that will take my mind off my worries. Or
let me get out and play a round of golf, or go to a
movie; that will help me ease the emptiness inside. Or why not just sit and stare at the television
for a while; it will dull the pain of my quarrels with
my children, my husband, my wife." These are the
escapes people use to try to get away from their
daily torments, but evading problems does not
solve them. Those troubles will beset a person all
the days of his life until he faces them and says:
"Now I am going to do something about them."

No one would try to cure drug addiction by
giving the addict more of his drug. Likewise, the
cure for the soul-starved restlessness addict is not
more restless diversion; it is meditation — immers-

ing body, mind, and emotions in the stillness and divine contentment within.

Most shun meditation not because they truly have no time, but because they do not want to face themselves — a definite result of the interiorization of meditation. There is too much they do not like in themselves, so they would rather keep the mind busy on externals, never thinking too deeply about the self-improvements they need to make. Get away from such mental laziness. Mental sloth, Patanjali pointed out in his *Yoga Sutras,* is one of the major obstacles that hinder our spiritual progress. It makes us say, "Well, tomorrow I will think of You, God. Today I am just too busy with the worries You have given me." Millions through the ages have made the same weak, lame excuse. What a delusive thought it is! "I want You, God, but tomorrow — as soon as I get my schedule under control—I will begin to think of You." That tomorrow will never come so long as you accept excuses. How many skulls have been strewn across the sands of time of individuals who had the intention to change themselves but not the discipline to do something about it now.

The tragedy of complacency is that most persons do not begin to do something about bettering their spiritual condition until their hearts are wrung with torment, sadness, frustration, suffering. Only then do they turn toward seeking the Divine. Why wait and go through such anguish? It is so simple to feel God now if we make but a little effort in meditation.

LIVE WITH DELIGHT

How marvelously different and fulfilling is the balanced life in God shown us by Paramahansa Yogananda: "Divine Mother,* teach me to live with delight. May I enjoy my earthly duties and the countless beauties of creation. Help me to train my senses to observe and appreciate Thy wondrous world of Nature. Let me savor with Thy zest all innocent pleasures. Save me from negation and unwarranted kill-joy attitudes."

This particularly appeals to me: "Let me savor with Thy zest all innocent pleasures." People have the notion that when you seek God, you have to be oh so solemn! But such false piety is not of the soul. The several saints I have met and associated with, including Paramahansaji, have been joyous, spontaneous, childlike. I do not mean childish — immature, irresponsible; I mean childlike — one who can enjoy the simplest pleasures, who lives with delight. Today in Western civilization people do not know how to enjoy simple things. They have become so jaded in their tastes that nothing satisfies: overstimulated outwardly, starved and empty inwardly, they take to drink or drugs to es-

---

* The Divine Mother is the aspect of God that is active in creation; the *shakti,* or power, of the Transcendent Creator. Also, the personal aspect of God as Mother, embodying the Lord's love and compassionate qualities. The Hindu scriptures teach that God is both immanent and transcendent, personal and impersonal. He may be sought as the Absolute; as one of His manifest eternal qualities, such as love, wisdom, bliss, light; or in a concept such as Heavenly Father, Mother, Friend.

cape. The values of contemporary culture are unhealthy, unnatural; that is why it fails to produce many truly balanced individuals and families that do not go to pieces. And it is not only in this country; that value-sickness is spreading in all countries, even in India.

Let us get back to the simple pleasures of life. Have you ever on your day off, for example, taken a drive up into the mountains, or out into the desert or some other quiet place, had a picnic, sat quietly, and thought about God? These are real pleasures; what joy they bring once you have cultivated the sensitivity of appreciating the Lord's presence in the beauty of nature. Just looking out over the ocean, or at some other natural panorama — even beautiful grass, beautiful trees — I get such a thrill from it. That we all can do.

You might say, "Well, it would be terribly boring." But just try it once instead of going to a movie, from which you usually return restless and moody. You wanted to enjoy it, but it did not make you happy. Instead, seek natural places of beauty and solitude and listen to the still voice of God speaking through His creation. What peace it will bring to you!

One who is seeking to know God must practice more stillness in his life — for at least a short time each day in meditation; for a few hours on the weekend, perhaps when you get out in nature; and for several days or a week every so often. It is usually not feasible to have lengthy periods of si-

lence and seclusion in family homes, and that is
why our Guru spoke of the importance of taking
retreats — to go someplace where you can be quiet
and refocus your life. He recognized that if people
would know God, they need to get away from the
pressures of their everyday environment, to come
to places where they can forget worldly cares,
worries, problems, desires, at least for a weekend,
and devote themselves exclusively to the thought
of God. I urge you to make spiritual retreats a part
of your life.

In dedicating our Encinitas Ashram Center
Paramahansaji spoke of it as "a place where one
can learn to feel the Fatherhood of God and acknowledge the brotherhood of man." He started
our first SRF Retreat in Encinitas as a place to foster that balanced lifestyle and those spiritual values
most needed if the nations of the world are to co-
exist peacefully.*

It is unrealistic to talk about peace among nations if the people in those nations are not at peace.
And they cannot be at peace with their neighbors
— or even with the members of their own household — if they are not at peace with themselves. It
has to begin with the individual. One of the first
questions people in every country have asked me
in my travels around the world is, "How can I find
peace?" I say to them: "There is no other way ex-

---

* The Self-Realization Fellowship Ashram Center and Retreat in Encinitas, California, overlooking the Pacific Ocean north of San Diego, was
founded by Paramahansa Yogananda in 1936.

cept by going within into the presence of God." Daily meditation — the foundation of this teaching brought by Paramahansa Yogananda — is the way to restore spiritual balance in the lives of pressured individuals and fractured families, and to resurrect those values that will nurture peace and harmony in the large household of our world family.

PART II:

THE NEW HARMONY BETWEEN SCIENCE AND SPIRITUALITY

Practicing Religion
Scientifically

Yoga or Modern Science?

Kriya Yoga: Spiritual Science
for an Awakening Age

Charles P. Steinmetz [1865-1923], the great electrical engineer, was once asked: "What line of research will see the greatest development during the next fifty years?" "I think the greatest discovery will be made along spiritual lines," Steinmetz replied. "Here is a force which history clearly teaches has been the greatest power in the development of men. Yet we have merely been playing with it and have never seriously studied it as we have the physical forces. Someday people will learn that material things do not bring happiness and are of little use in making men and women creative and powerful. Then the scientists of the world will turn their laboratories over to the study of God and prayer and the spiritual forces which as yet have hardly been scratched. When this day comes, the world will see more advancement in one generation than it has seen in the past four."

> —*quoted in Paramahansa Yogananda's*
> Autobiography of a Yogi

PRACTICING RELIGION
SCIENTIFICALLY

By Paramahansa Yogananda

It is often said that there is a great conflict between science and religion. It is true that scientists look doubtfully at the scriptural statement that "the heaven and the earth" were created
in a matter of days. From their practical studies of
the earth and the heavens, they have proved that
creation came into being through a slow evolutionary process; and that the progression of earth
alone, from gases to matter, plants, animal life, and
man, required millions of years. So there is a great
deal of difference between the findings of the scientists and a literal interpretation of the scriptural
texts.

One of the virtues of the true scientist is that he
is open-minded. Working from a little data, he ex-

*Extracts from a talk given at Self-Realization Fellowship Temple,
Encinitas, California, February 18, 1940. The complete talk is pub-
lished in* The Divine Romance (Collected Talks and Essays, Volume
II) *by Paramahansa Yogananda (Los Angeles: Self-Realization
Fellowship).*

periments until he uncovers verifiable principles of nature and how they work; then he gives to the world the result of his investigations. And he is willing to consider and to research further any new evidence that comes to light. It is the efforts of such scientists that have resulted in the discovery of all the natural laws that have been harnessed for the benefit of the world today. Gradually we are learning to use these laws in an ever-widening range of practical ways; as for example in the numerous conveniences in our homes.

SCIENTISTS WORK IN COOPERATION WITH GOD

Scientists are often branded as materially minded because of their questioning of unproved religious beliefs. But God does not condemn them for that. His universal laws operate with impartial justice regardless of man's beliefs. In this sense God is not a respecter of persons but a respecter of law. He has given us free will, and whether we worship Him or not, if we respect His laws, we shall receive the beneficial results of such regard. A doubting scientist might explain his position in this way: "Even if I don't believe in God, I do try to do what is right. If there is a God, He will reward or punish me according to my respect for His laws. And if there is no God, since I am obeying the laws I find to be true, surely I shall receive any benefit therefrom."

So, whether or not they are godless, or making

their efforts for material gain, those scientists whose researches are uncovering more and more of God's laws are nonetheless working in cooperation with Him to do some good for the world.

BELIEF IS ONLY THE FIRST STEP

Law governs everything in the universe; yet most people have never tried to apply the scientific law of experimentation and research to test religious doctrines. They simply believe, thinking it impossible to investigate and prove the scriptural texts. "We have only to believe," they assure themselves and others; and that is to be accepted as all there is to religion. But the Bible tells us that "Faith is the *substance* of things hoped for, the *evidence* of things not seen."* Faith is different from belief, which is only the first step. If I were to tell you that behind this building there is a huge lion, you would probably say, "We don't see how it could be possible!" But if I insisted, "Yes, there is a lion there," you would believe me to the extent that you would go out and investigate. Belief was necessary in order to make you look into it — and if you didn't see the lion, you would say that I had told you a story! Similarly, if I want to persuade you to make a spiritual experiment, you have to believe me before you will carry it out. You can believe, at least, until you prove differently.

* Hebrews 11:1.

Faith, however, cannot be contradicted: it is intuitive conviction of truth, and it cannot be shaken even by contrary evidence. Faith can heal the sick, raise the dead, create new universes. Jesus said, "If ye have faith as a grain of mustard seed, ye shall say unto this mountain, Remove hence to yonder place; and it shall remove; and nothing shall be impossible unto you."*

Science is reasonable, willing to alter its views in the light of new facts. It is skeptical about religion only because it has not experimented in that field; although it is now beginning such research at Harvard. Experimental psychology has greatly advanced, and is doing its utmost to understand the inner man. Machines have been invented that can record the different kinds of emotion man experiences; it is said that if one lies while being tested on a polygraph, he usually cannot conceal the fact, no matter how hard he tries.

Self-realization Is Necessary to Experience God

Scientific knowledge is built upon facts. The medical side is fairly well developed, though the causes and cures of certain ailments are yet to be discovered. But what science does know, it is more or less sure about, because the various factors concerned have been tested: theories have

* Matthew 17:20.

been tried and proven. In religion it is different. People are given certain facts or truths and told to believe them. After a little while, when their belief is not fulfilled, doubt creeps in; and then they go from religion to religion trying to find proof. You hear about God in churches and temples; you can read about Him in books; but you can *experience* God only through Self-realization attained by practicing definite scientific techniques. In India, religion is based upon such scientific methods. Realization is what India specialized in, and those who want to know God should learn her methods; they are not India's sole property. Just as electricity was discovered in the West, and we in India benefit from it; so India has discovered the ways by which God can be known, and the West should profit by them. By experimentation, India has proved the truths in religion. In the future, religion everywhere will be a matter of experimentation; it will not be based solely upon belief.

Millions of people are changing from one church to another without truly believing in their hearts what they have heard about God. They say, "Well, I pray, but most of the time He does not respond." Nevertheless, God is always aware of us. He knows all about us, yet we remain absolutely ignorant of Him. This is the cause of the various kinds of doubts that play upon our minds. If God is, we must be able to know Him. Why should we merely read and hear discussions about Him, and yet know nothing from personal experience?

Yet there is a definite way to experience God. And what is that way? It is scientific experimentation with religious truths. And put into practice what you believe! It is possible to put religion into practice, to use it as a science that you can prove by experimenting on yourself. The search for Truth is the most marvelous search in the world. Instead of being merely a matter of attending a Sunday service or performing one's *puja*,* religion must have a practical side. Learn how to build your life around spiritual ideals. Without practical application, religion is of little value....

So religion must be experimented with, to prove it and make it practical. Many churches do great social good, but they do not show you how you can actually prove God to yourself, and how you can be in tune with Him.

If you haven't felt any results from religion, experiment in meditation. Shake God out of His silence. You must insist: "Lord, speak to me!" If you make a supreme effort in the silence of the night and in the early morning, after a little while you will see a glimmer of God's light or feel a ripple of His joy coming over your consciousness. Experimenting to know God in meditation, in silence, brings the most real, most remarkable results.

Scientists once thought that water was a single element. But experiments later proved that two invisible elements, hydrogen and oxygen, come to-

---

* Ritual worship performed by Hindus.

gether in a certain combination to make up water. Similarly, by religious experiment, wonderful spiritual truths are realized. When you sit quietly in meditation, and your mind is withdrawn within, you will have proof of God and of your own true nature. Experimentation with religious laws is marvelous because the result doesn't take place outside yourself; it is right within you....

THE SCIENCE OF RELIGION

Everything that is visible is the result of the Invisible. Because you do not see God, you do not believe He is here. Yet every tree and every blade of grass is controlled by the power of God within it. That Power is not visible externally. What you see are merely the results coming from the Power in the seeds planted in the earth, which emerge as the tree and the blades of grass. You do not see what is going on within, in the factory of the Infinite. Every object in this universe, and every potential therein, has been produced first in the factory of the mind of God; and God sublets that power to the factory of the mind of man. From that little factory of man's mind comes everything he accomplishes — great books, intricate machines, outstanding achievements in any walk of life. Above all, in that mind-factory lies man's unique ability to find God.

The mind is a perfect instrument of knowledge when you have learned to base your life on truth.

Then you see everything in a clear, undistorted way, exactly as it is. Therefore, learn to experiment with this mind. Learn to follow the science of religion and you can become the greatest kind of scientist, the greatest kind of inventor, the master of your own fate.

If you can just remember and apply the truths I have told you, there is nothing you cannot accomplish in life. And the greatest of all achievements is to find God. By the application of science in religion, your uncertain belief in spiritual possibilities can become realization of their highest fulfillment. Then you will be the most successful of all human beings, greater than all the scientists on earth. The great ones who have discovered Him never live in doubt; they experience the truth. "Ye shall know the truth, and the truth shall make you free."*

* John 8:32.

Yoga or Modern Science?

By Tara Mata

Material science is more theoretical than true religion. Science is able to investigate, for example, the external nature and behavior of the atom. But the practice of meditation bestows omnipresence; a yogi can become one with the atom.—Paramahansa Yogananda

Modern inventions merely copy nature. The telescope is only equivalent to a pair of abnormally bright eyes and brings us merely an extension of vision. It cannot give us a new sense but simply enlarges the sense of sight we already possess. Knowledge of the electromagnetic world of atomic structure has opened to us universes so infinitely small that the microscope itself cannot perceive them and we must represent them with mathematical equations.* But we understand that, given a microscope of sufficient power, the atoms, being forms, could be seen. We see light, though it travels 186,000 miles a second. We see the An-

* This article was written in the early 1930s, before invention of the electron microscope.

dromeda Galaxy, and the inconceivably distant universes of stars, with the naked eye.

Because we cannot go beyond sensory perception (for even thought and imagination are forms perceived with the inward eye or the inward sight), the ancient Hindus, and doubtless every other great race of the past Golden Ages, built up their systems of mental science, Yoga (control), through which the senses were refined, broadened, and sharpened so that all natural phenomena lay open to their true-seeing gaze.

INNER SIGHT NEEDS NO SPECTACLES

The whole body of scientific inventions that represents the genius of man at our present stage in this new cycle of upward evolution was unnecessary — like spectacles on a man of good vision — to Golden Age *rishis* (literally, seers). Red begins the spectrum of colors, and red ends it, but the intensity of one is not the intensity of the other. Though it is true that extremes seem to meet, and that both the most backward peoples, and those belonging to the highest civilizations, do not have inventions and observatories and scientific laboratories, yet in the first case it is due to the ignorance of Kali Yuga (Dark Age), and in the latter case to the perfected insight of Golden Age men. So we need not conclude, because the ancients left no records of inventions such as we have today, that they were ignorant men. Inventions are for Dwapara and Treta

Yugas (the Bronze and Silver Ages), the midpoints between savagery and true civilization.

Thinkers of our own age are not failing to point out that our inventions are likely to lead us to ruin unless and until we are morally developed enough to direct and use them rightly. Without a better understanding of his own nature, man is unprepared for the responsibility of a knowledge of nature and her dynamic forces. So the Golden Age men developed and perfected a science of man—Yoga—not a science of nature, for that follows automatically.

MAN IS A UNIVERSE

Man too is a solar system, a universe, fit for the profoundest study. He too has a Grand Central Sun within him, the Spiritual Sun. He too is a Creator and by him creation was made, is preserved, and shall be destroyed—the trinity of all religions. Yet what does he know of himself? Man can harness the lightning, tame the wind and control the elements, pluck the moon from the sky and bring it to his own doorstep with his telescopes more easily than he can control his own passions. Yet that was the goal and the achievement of Golden Age men, the "gods" of all ancient mythologies.

Out of millions a Newton and an Einstein are born, with enough natural concentration to penetrate some of the secrets of nature. These men are true men; Newton was deeply religious, and Einstein was a true humanitarian. But the results of their research, the host of practical inventions that follows each new discovery of the laws of nature — can these be entrusted to the hands of ordinary men? Are not discoveries in physics and chemistry too often put to destructive use, as in war? There have always been spiritually undeveloped men who use technology and inventions to enslave others, and the machine age is far from a perfect one.

Such are the dangers of inventions. The forces of nature are not for the use of those lacking in true wisdom. First perfect the man, then he will know how to utilize nature. We do not need to perfect a cosmic-ray method of curing cancer, if we produce a race of men of pure minds and bodies where no cancer can grow. Man is the problem, not nature.

The more we discover of natural laws and their practical utilization, the more quickly we will see that without a corresponding extension of knowledge of man and his own nature and its control, the specter of worldwide destruction is the only promise of the future.

World Conditions Reflect the Temper of Man

World peace is only the dream of visionaries so long as man does not know and is not taught how to control his passions. Whether he fights with poison gas or from the air with bombs, or with his

bare hands, he is still a victim of his own ignorance. If he can live at peace and in harmony and
cooperation with his family, his neighbors, and his
friends, then he is fit for world peace. When nations are composed of men like that, then we can
expect world peace. Man is the measure of all
things, according to the Hermetic teachings and all
ancient philosophies. World conditions can do no
more than reflect the temper of man.

It was for this reason that Krishna, Buddha,
Christ, all the great teachers of mankind, stressed
one point and only one — the conquering of human passions. They did not attack institutions nor
initiate sweeping outward reforms of social or economic conditions, because these are only an effect
of far deeper causes. The sages who have guided
mankind did not bring inventions with them nor
point out new ways to enslave nature for the daily
purposes of man. The conquest of the internal nature should be the primary occupation for a human
being. Otherwise he is no higher than an animal.

Spiders can spin a geometric web; the ant is the
greatest organizer in the world. A monkey can put
any agile athlete to shame; the hibernating animals
can live without food or drink; a turtle can exist for
hundreds of years. A body of strength and endur-
ance is not the measure of a man, nor his command
of mathematics nor the extent of his scientific or
artistic ingenuity. The measure of a man is his control over himself — his lower self, his thoughts, his
impulses, his desires, and his actions. This goal can

never be achieved without a knowledge of his own nature, such as is embodied in the psychological, mental, and spiritual sciences of Yoga. These sciences all rest on the same fundamental foundation of morality (*yama* and *niyama*), nonstealing, noninjury, truthfulness, etc. This is the starting point of all religions as they were laid down by their founders.

FALLIBILITY OF SCIENCE

Science such as we know it today is fallible. There is no such thing as certainty or finality, when the proof must depend on the ordinary perceptive sensory powers of man. If the sensory instruments are faulty, so will be conclusions. And all inventions depend on the senses of man to utilize them.

Golden Age men therefore set out to perfect their sensory instruments, and did it so well that there is no modern discovery of natural law that has not already been known and elucidated by the ancients. What fragments of natural laws have been discovered through physical instruments by the moderns were known, and far more comprehensively, by the ancients without any other instrument than their true inward eye.

Modern science will ultimately confirm what the ancients have already said about the nature of the universe. But the conclusions of scientists will still be minus the ring of conviction, for knowledge obtained by outward means can never fully satisfy the nature of man, and there is always an element of doubt connected with every man-given dictum. The foremost scientists of our time openly acknowledge that they expect their present views to be overturned by later developments. But the ancient *rishis knew,* because they had *seen,* and not merely arrived at their conclusions by the trial-and-error method. Hence they could sing of the laws of the universe, could mix science and poetry and music, as later Pythagoras did, with the utmost serenity, knowing that future ages could do no more than confirm the timeless truths they were giving out.

Kriya Yoga: Spiritual Science for an Awakening Age

By Brother Achalananda

More than seventy years have passed since Paramahansa Yogananda was sent from India to the West to disseminate the ancient science of Kriya Yoga worldwide.* At the time, few people realized the significance of what he was bringing; but if we look back at the incredible transformations that have occurred in the years since then, we can see that Kriya Yoga was introduced to the world at a particular time for a very definite reason.

Environment, Economy, and Ethics

Commenting on the complex patterns of change now sweeping our planet, a columnist for *The Christian Science Monitor* recently had this to say:

Spotting trends is never easy, especially in midstream. Sometimes they ambush you, as with the

---

* Paramahansaji arrived in Boston on September 19, 1920.

sudden collapse of East-bloc communism. Sometimes you get plenty of signals but can't interpret them, as when the current statistics on drug use suggest both growth and decline. So, at the risk of spotting a false trend or misreading a real one, let me offer a characterization of the 1990s as the "E" decade. That stands for economy, environment, and ethics. Those three things, once separate, are rapidly lining up on the same side....A healthy economy depends on a healthy ecology. ...[and] we're increasingly aware that our environment and our economy depend on our ethics —our sense of right and wrong, our deepest human values.*

This points toward an extremely important truth: The myriad social, political, moral, and personal crises our world is facing cannot be solved separately, for in reality they are different expressions of the same underlying cause. Modern science is radically transforming our lives, but until we also develop the inner side of our being—our moral and spiritual faculties—we will not be able to use our technological advancements with wisdom and compassion. And though many writers and social observers have noted that this is the fundamental crisis of our age, very few have been able to explain why it came about or how to solve it.

Persons of deep spiritual insight, however, fully understand what is taking place. From astronomical references in ancient Hindu texts that have

* Rushworth M. Kidder, March 19, 1990.

been handed down from the higher ages, Paramahansa Yogananda's guru, Swami Sri Yukteswar, cal-
culated that the lowest point in the current 24,000-
year cycle occurred just before A.D. 500. In that
year, the upward arc of the cycle began, leading
humanity through 1,200 years of the ascending
Kali Yuga to the advent of Dwapara Yuga at the
end of the 1600s. That marked the beginning of a
200-year transition period into ascending Dwapara
Yuga; the beginning of Dwapara Yuga proper occurred at the dawn of the twentieth century.*

ENERGY: CENTRAL INFLUENCE ON HUMAN CIVILIZATION TODAY

Now, this whole subject of the *yugas* is a vast
and complex one. I mention only these basic
points to help us understand the incredible transformation that has occurred in the twentieth century. Civilization has changed more in the past
hundred years than in the previous two thousand.
Why did this come about? With the dawn of Dwapara Yuga, man began to understand that the material world, which seemed so solid and real to his
Kali Yuga ancestors, is in reality nothing but an expression of energy — electrical patterns, tiny scin-
tillating points of light dancing in and out of material manifestation on the vast "stage" of the
quantum field.

* See page 8.

This emerging understanding of energy, and its technological application, is the central influence on the evolution of human civilization today. As Swami Sri Yukteswar predicted, our harnessing of the electrical and atomic forces is gradually giving us the power to annihilate the barriers of space. Already we see this to some degree: The earth, which seemed so huge to our grandparents, can now be circumnavigated in less than an hour by spacecraft, and in a fraction of a second we can send communications anywhere in the world. Those enormous distances have for all practical purposes disappeared. In 1903, just a few years after the dawn of the new age, the Wright brothers flew the first plane that was heavier than air. They were able to fly a distance of just over 100 feet. Yet less than seventy years later we were sending people to the moon; and the 100 feet of that first flight is less than the wingspan of the large passenger aircraft that are common today. Computers, telecommunications, advanced medical technologies — the results of the fantastic explosion of ability that has taken place in the past few decades have revolutionized our lives.

Why Do People Today Feel Such Pressure?

However, lately some of the "benefits" of science have begun to seem more and more disconcerting! In contrast to the popular assumption that technology would change our economy so much that we would be able to live lives of leisure, consider this report from *Time* magazine, April 24, 1989:

> In 1967, testimony before a Senate subcommittee indicated that by 1985 people could be working just 22 hours a week or 27 weeks a year or could retire at 38. That would leave only the great challenge of finding a way to enjoy all that leisure. And not only would the office be transformed. The American household soaked up microwaves, VCRs, blow dryers, mix 'n' eat, the computerized automobile....The kitchen was streamlined with so much labor-saving gadgetry that meals could be prepared, served, and cleaned up in less time than it took to boil an egg. Thus freed from household chores, Mom could head off to a committee meeting on social justice, while Dad chaired the men's-club clothing drive, and the kids went to bed at 10:30 after watching a PBS special on nuclear physics.
>
> Sure enough, the computers are byting, the satellites spinning, the Cuisinarts whizzing, just as planned. Yet we are ever out of breath....According to a Harris survey, the amount of leisure time enjoyed by the average American has shrunk 37% since 1973. Over the same period, the average workweek, including commuting, has jumped from under 41 hours to nearly 47 hours. In some professions, predictably law, finance, and medicine, the demands often stretch to 80-plus hours a week. Vacations have shortened to the point where they are frequently no more than long weekends. And the Sabbath is for — what else? — shopping.

Why are most people today in such a rush that they cannot even find time to relax and cultivate relationships with their spouse and children, much less with God? Economic reasons and the sheer complexity of modern life explain to a certain extent why people are so frantic, but beyond these is something deeper: the fact that their lifestyle leaves certain basic needs unfulfilled. By crowding their daily schedules with more work, more entertainment, more of all kinds of outer activity, people are desperately trying to find a way to fill the tremendous sense of emptiness they feel within.

When people direct all their attention and energies outwardly, they have no sense of the magnificent soul within; and without an awareness and expression of the spiritual side of their being, how can they feel good about themselves? The means of seeking outer pleasures and distractions have been multiplied a thousandfold by the technological avalanche of the last few decades. Do you think it is just coincidence that during this same period we have begun to hear for the first time that "low self-esteem" is becoming epidemic in our society?

The more our lives are bound by external pursuits of happiness, the less happiness we can hold onto. Satisfaction quickly goes, because there is always something "new" and "improved" to yearn for, increasing the feeling of lack. It is a vicious circle: the deeper our sense of nonfulfillment, the more frenzied our chase for some new possession or material achievement or experience that we hope will fill the inner void. This lifestyle is the source of un-believable pressure in the lives of millions today.

Life doesn't have to be that way. I remember my first meeting with Rajarsi Janakananda, in 1953.* Early in his life he had become very successful. However, even though he had been able to acquire all the material possessions that most people crave, he lived in a state of inner stress and nervousness. His health had suffered, and he became extremely unhappy. Then he met Paramahansaji and began to practice Kriya Yoga. Through Kriya and the bless-ings of the Master, Rajarsi had been transformed into a God-realized saint. I looked into his eyes and face, and there was such joy, such love and peace, emanating from him. I literally staggered away after receiving his blessing. And I thought, "I don't know what he has, but one thing I do know—I want it!"

KRIYA YOGA: THE SPIRITUAL APPLICATION OF ENERGY

You see, technology is not the cause of our prob-lems; unbalanced living is. There is a very hopeful side to the scientific understanding of energy that was ushered in with our awakening age: It made possible the reintroduction of the ancient science of Kriya Yoga, which was lost for centuries but which

* A highly advanced American yogi, Rajarsi Janakananda (James J. Lynn) was Paramahansa Yogananda's first spiritual successor as president of Self-Realization Fellowship. He served in that position from 1952 until his passing in 1955.

reappeared in the world at the dawn of the Atomic
Age (Dwapara Yuga). Just as modern civilization did
not become possible until man was able to comprehend the energies in creation, so the knowledge of
Kriya Yoga remained hidden for centuries because
people could not grasp the subtle forces on which
Kriya is based.*

Until man begins to employ a spiritual technique that is at least as powerful as his means of
applying energy in the outer world, he will grow
increasingly unbalanced, increasingly threatened
with personal distress and global disaster. Kriya
Yoga provides the "missing link" in our twentieth
century understanding of energy; it gives the
means to balance material progress with spiritual
development. In contrast to the outer technologies that enable us to harness the energies in our
external environment, we might say that Kriya
Yoga is an inner "technology" — the science of

---

* In *Autobiography of a Yogi,* Paramahansa Yogananda writes:

"Kriya is an ancient science. Lahiri Mahasaya received it [in 1861] from
his great guru, Babaji, who rediscovered and clarified the technique after
it had been lost in the Dark Ages. Babaji renamed it, simply, Kriya Yoga.

"'The Kriya Yoga that I am giving to the world through you in this nine-
teenth century,' Babaji told Lahiri Mahasaya, 'is a revival of the same science
that Krishna gave millenniums ago to Arjuna; and that was later known to
Patanjali and Christ, and to St. John, St. Paul, and other disciples.'

"Kriya Yoga is twice referred to by Lord Krishna, India's greatest
prophet, in the Bhagavad Gita....Krishna also relates that it was he, in a
former incarnation, who communicated the indestructible yoga to an ancient illuminato, Vivasvat, who gave it to Manu, the great legislator. He, in
turn, instructed Ikshwaku, founder of India's solar warrior dynasty. Passing thus from one to another, the royal yoga was guarded by the *rishis* until the coming of the materialistic ages. Then, because of priestly secrecy
and man's indifference, the sacred lore gradually became inaccessible."

controlling the energies of life and consciousness. In *The Science of Religion,* Paramahansaji explains how Kriya works with energy:

> The life-force generally goes outward, keeping the body and mind always in motion, and causing disturbances to the spiritual Self in the shape of bodily sensations and passing thoughts. Because the life-force moves outward, sensations and thoughts disturb and distort the calm image of the Self or Soul....
>
> [Kriya Yoga] teaches a process enabling us to draw to our *central part*—spine and brain—the life current distributed throughout the organs and other parts of our body. The process consists of magnetizing the spinal column and the brain, which contain the seven main centers [through which life energy flows outward into the body], with the result that the distributed life electricity is drawn back to the original centers of discharge and is experienced in the form of light. In this state the spiritual Self can consciously free itself from its bodily and mental distractions....
>
> The superiority of this method over others lies in the fact that it works with the exact thing that binds us down to our narrow individuality—the life-force....This method teaches us to turn the life-force inward. Hence it is direct and immediate. It takes us straight to the consciousness of Self—the Bliss-God.

"Man's forgetfulness of his divine resources (through misuse of free will) is the root cause of all other forms of suffering," Paramahansa Yogananda wrote. He tells us that no matter what type of problem was presented to Lahiri Mahasaya* by troubled souls who sought his blessing, he invariably counseled Kriya Yoga for its solution. Why? Because Kriya deals with the exact cause of our ignorance of our innate divinity: the uncontrolled outward flow of life energy and consciousness.

RESTORING ECOLOGICAL BALANCE IN OUR PLANETARY ENVIRONMENT

The fact that most people are unaware of their divine nature is nothing new; this has been the condition of human society for thousands of years, since the last higher age. During Kali Yuga this posed no great threat to the survival of the planet, but the situation takes on critical importance in this era of rapidly developing technology. Writing in the *Los Angeles Times* (March 7, 1990) biology professor Charles Birch, Ph.D., said:

> Our technological civilization has not adapted to the needs of survival....There is something radically wrong with the way we are living on Earth today. The sort of society we are building with the aid of science and technology has self-destructive features built into it.... Each year man annihilates at least 1,000 species that share the planet with us. This is nothing less than a holocaust of nature.

* A seminal figure in the renaissance of yoga in modern India. The life of this great master is described in *Autobiography of a Yogi.*

Do you know why the very ability of the earth to sustain life is threatened today? Because underlying the West's rise to technological and economic supremacy is an exploitative mindset — one that has evolved through a complete misunderstanding of the scriptures that are the basis of our fundamental values. Take, for example, this passage from the Bible (Genesis 1:26):

> And God said, "Let us make man in our image, after our likeness: and let them have dominion over the fish of the sea, and over the fowl of the air, and over the cattle, and over all the earth, and over every creeping thing that creepeth upon the earth."

Paramahansaji tells us that the Bible never meant that human beings were to exploit the earth in order to gratify their material desires. The true significance of this scriptural passage is much deeper — an exhortation to all human beings to throw off the thralldom of *maya,* the world delusion that keeps us in bondage to our mortal nature. "For this purpose were man and creation made," Paramahansaji writes, "that he should rise up as master of *maya,* knowing his dominion over the cosmos."

"Total spiritual confusion prevails in the modern world about the relationship of humanity to nature in a technological culture," Professor Birch continues. "Western religious thought is most weak here, where the ache of the world is most strong. The whole of creation cries out in agony for liberation. Can religions remain silent on this agony much longer?"

Here is where Kriya Yoga provides an answer that is as beautiful as it is complete. In *Autobiography of a Yogi,* Paramahansaji quotes Ananda Mohan Lahiri, the grandson of Lahiri Mahasaya:

> Our eagerness for worldly activity kills in us the sense of spiritual awe. Because modern science tells us how to utilize the powers of Nature, we fail to comprehend the Great Life in back of all names and forms. Familiarity with Nature has bred contempt for her ultimate secrets; our relation with her is one of practical business. We tease her, so to speak, to discover the ways in which she may be forced to serve our purposes; we make use of her energies, whose Source yet remains unknown. In science our relation with Nature is like that between an arrogant man and his servant; or, in a philosophical sense, Nature is like a captive in the witness box. We cross-examine her, challenge her, and minutely weigh her evidence in human scales that cannot measure her hidden values.
>
> On the other hand, when the self is in communion with a higher power, Nature automatically obeys, without stress or strain, the will of man. This effortless command over Nature is called "miraculous" by the uncomprehending materialist.... In spite of the matter-of-factness of physical science, every man may find a way through Kriya Yoga to understand his proper relation with Nature and to feel spiritual reverence for all phenomena, whether mystical or of everyday occurrence.

KRIYA HELPS US CHANGE OURSELVES— AND THE WORLD

> "The movement to a lasting society cannot oc-
> cur without a transformation of individual val-
> ues and priorities....Materialism simply cannot
> survive the transition to a sustainable world."
> —*Worldwatch, "State of the World Report," 1990*

The more deeply we analyze the problems our
world is facing, the more we understand that their
root is not political or social, but moral and spiritual. Paramahansaji wrote in his *Autobiography of
a Yogi:*

> The Western day is nearing when the inner sci-
> ence of self-control will be found as necessary
> as the outer conquest of Nature. The Atomic
> Age will see men's minds sobered and broad-
> ened by the now scientifically indisputable truth
> that matter is in reality a concentrate of energy.
> The human mind can and must liberate within
> itself energies greater than those within stones
> and metals, lest the material atomic giant, newly
> unleashed, turn on the world in mindless de-
> struction. An indirect benefit of mankind's con-
> cern over atomic bombs may be an increased
> practical interest in the science of yoga, a
> "bombproof shelter" truly.

More and more people are realizing that our
highest priority should be to find God. In finding
Him within ourselves, we begin to see the same
God in everyone. We begin to behave as brothers
and sisters and friends toward one another, and to-

ward the planet that sustains us. To awaken that consciousness is the role of Kriya Yoga.

On the eve of Paramahansaji's departure for America in 1920, Mahavatar Babaji said to him: "Kriya Yoga, the scientific technique of God-realization, will ultimately spread in all lands, and aid in harmonizing the nations through man's personal, transcendental perception of the Infinite Father." Kriya can awaken within each of us the love of God, which is so wonderful that once we perceive it we want to express it in all of our dealings with the world.

The inner spiritual transformation of people is the only way to change this world. Peace pacts will not do it; we cannot change people by passing laws. There was an ordinance at Gettysburg that made it illegal to discharge firearms there, but that didn't prevent the bloodiest battle of the Civil War. Real change can come only from the moral and spiritual efforts of individuals. As the Scottish philosopher Carlyle said, "Change yourself, and then you will know there is at least one less rascal in the world!" In Kriya Yoga we have been given the means to change ourselves.

Like all the other major social problems of our era, the moral crisis is in essence an "energy crisis." As long as all our life energy is consumed in the world of the senses, our consciousness remains oblivious to the infinite stores of wisdom, bliss, and divine love that lie at the innermost core of our being. But through continued practice of Kriya, the whole focus of our life changes.

PERSEVERE IN YOUR PRACTICE

As we faithfully practice these teachings, we see that slowly, day by day, we do change for the better. We have beautiful examples of the efficacy of this holy science, not only in our Guru, but in his great disciples—Rajarsi Janakananda, for example; and our current president, Sri Daya Mata. All over the world I have seen souls who are making tremendous spiritual progress through the practice of Kriya. Some may be in positions where they are observed; others are not. Sometimes the changes come quickly, and sometimes they take longer to become apparent. This should not matter to us. What is important is that each of us keep making a continuous effort to experience what Kriya can do for us. If we persevere in our practice, we can be sure that we will get the exact results the Guru has promised, and we will find that transformation of consciousness which is the most urgent need on our planet today.

Let me conclude by quoting Paramahansaji's words:

> I have been practicing [Kriya Yoga] for many years, and the more I do so, the more I feel the joy of a state of permanent and unfailing Bliss.
>
> We should bear in mind that the spiritual Self has been in bondage to the body for how many ages we know not. It may not be freed in one day, nor will short or desultory practice of the method take one to the supreme state of Bliss....It may require patient practice for a long, long time.

This can be guaranteed, however, that the following of this process will bring the great joy of pure Bliss-consciousness. The more we practice it, the more quickly we attain Bliss. I wish that, as seekers of Bliss, which all of us are, you would try to experience for yourselves that universal truth which is in all and may be felt by all. This state is not an invention of anyone. It is already there; we have simply to discover it.

PART III
THE NEW RELIGION

The Need for Universal Religious Principles

*"One World": Expanding the Boundaries
of Our Love and Friendship*

Yoga: The Science of Religion

Unless a balance is created by developing spiritual realization along with advancement of the physical sciences, individuals and nations will be lost in misery and destruction. If today's world leaders were illumined by Self-realization, and worked together, they could within a few years banish war and poverty from the earth. Only spiritual consciousness—realization of God's presence in oneself and in every other living being—can save the world. I see no chance for peace without it. Begin with yourself. There is no time to waste. It is your duty to do your part to bring God's kingdom on earth.

—*Paramahansa Yogananda,*
in Man's Eternal Quest

THE NEED FOR UNIVERSAL
RELIGIOUS PRINCIPLES
REPLY TO QUESTIONS OF A TRUTH SEEKER

BY PARAMAHANSA YOGANANDA

Extracts from an interview conducted in 1951 by Professor Bhagwat S. Upadhyaya, distinguished author and historian of Indian culture. The complete interview is published in *Journey to Self-realization: Discovering the Gifts of the Soul (Collected Talks and Essays, Volume III)* by Paramahansa Yogananda (Los Angeles: Self-Realization Fellowship).

You are a man of religion; but don't you think that religion has been a cause of division, bloodshed, and evil in the world?

The existence of imitation gold does not decrease the value of pure gold. Similarly, spurious religion does not diminish the worth of true religion. Those who abuse the power of religion or who only pretend to follow religious practices for their own self-promotion become hypocrites and are sometimes perpetrators of evil; they are the wrong-doers, not religion. Those who exemplify true religion, or *dharma,* are a source of upliftment to the world; and they themselves become forever free from sorrow. True religion consists of those principles by which body, mind, and soul can be united to God. It is ultimately the only savior that can rescue man from all the evils of the earth.

Is religion per se really necessary for the upliftment of man? When he joins a particular faith or order, does he not rather circumscribe himself and thus create barriers between himself and those of other creeds?

Dogmatic religions are bypaths, sometimes blind alleys leading nowhere; but even so, a fairly good dogmatic religion can lead the sincere seeker to the highway of true religion, which in turn leads to God. That highway is yoga, the scientific process by which every soul reunites with Spirit. In the Bhagavad Gita, yoga is proclaimed greater than all other paths — greater than those of devotion, wisdom, and righteous action. Yoga is the science of how man descended from Spirit into flesh and became identified with the body and its senses and possessions; and how he can reascend to God. The experience, or realization, of truth that comes from yoga practice provides proof of the underlying unity of all religions found in the perception of their one common denominator — God.

Should religion take the form of an organized entity, such as Buddhism or Christianity, or should it rather be one of individual intuitive faith?

Organized religion is the hive; realization is the honey. Both are necessary. But it often happens that when organized religion concentrates on the outward tenets and ceremonial aspects it becomes a dogmatic empty hive. At the opposite extreme, some yogis in the Himalayas gather the honey of God-realization in their hearts without providing hives of organized religion through which others might share that divine nectar. That is selfish. If organized religion is backed by great savants, it does much good in the world. If it is promoted only by egotistical, bigoted, or commercial people, it does little good and often much harm to people in general.

If faith be intuitive, will it even then need a guru?

God does not talk openly to novitiate spiritual seekers; their intuition is not yet developed, and so inner guidance is not infallible. God therefore guides through the instructions of a guru who communes with Him. The preceptor must have divine attunement or we have "the blind leading the blind."

Does not religion take the form of a dogma after it is organized and defined by symbols and conventions?

Just as the nut is hidden within the shell, so is true religion hidden in the distorting dogmatic formalities of religion. But as a nutshell can be opened by a nutcracker and the meat found inside, so deep spiritual seekers, by the nutcracker of intuitive meditation on religious ideals, can break the dogmatic shell and get at the inner hidden truth. A crow may peck vainly at a hard walnut shell and never get at the meat; similarly, shallow spiritual seekers bite unsuccessfully at the dogmatic shell of religion without ever getting to the kernel of truth.

You believe there is a fundamental unity of all religions. If that be so, why is there jealousy and conflict between the followers of one creed and those of other persuasions?

We read of such conflicts even in the ancient scriptures. The disciples of the great god Shiva extol him as supreme; the Vaishnavites consider Vishnu and his incarnations as Rama or Krishna to be the highest. Worshipers within the divisions of religion have not the full realization of those whose lives have inspired true paths. I have often said that if Jesus, Krishna, Buddha, and other true emissaries of God came together, they would not quarrel, but would drink from the same one cup of God-communion.

The varying views of religionists are akin to the story told in India about six blind brothers who were washing an elephant. The first brother proclaimed that the elephant is like a huge wall; he had been washing the sides of the pachyderm. Hearing this, the second brother disagreed, asserting that the elephant is like a flexible bamboo pole; he had been washing the trunk. The third, thinking those two brothers were fools, insisted that the elephant is like two banana leaves; he had been washing the ears. Hearing these absurd pronouncements, the fourth brother corrected them with his definition that the elephant is like a large fleshy roof supported by four pillars; he had been washing the legs. The fifth brother laughed derisively, for to him the elephant was just two pieces of bone; he had been washing the tusks. Now the sixth brother knew they were all crazy and declared definitely that the elephant was only a piece of rope hanging from heaven; he had washed the tail and, being the youngest and small-est, he couldn't reach the top of the tail and so as-sumed it descended from the celestial regions of the gods. At the height of the quarrel, their sighted fa-ther arrived and explained, "You are all right, and you are all wrong. Right, because you correctly de-scribed what you experienced, but wrong because each of you experienced only a part of the whole. The elephant is an aggregate of all of these parts."

Man's consciousness evolves through incarna-tions and gradually experiences more and more of the nectar-ocean of truth. Each person can absorb only to the degree of his individual experience. These differences in perception are the cause of arguments and controversies, each seeing only a part of the whole truth. An exchange of differing views is constructive if done with openness and respect; but destructive, ending in quarrels, if there is bigotry and fanaticism.

＊

Do you find similarities between the Hindu and Christian faiths?

The Bhagavad Gita and the Christian Bible, especially the New Testament, I consider the greatest of all scriptures because they both point out the same yoga highway to God. The Bhagavad Gita teaches: "He is a man of realization who sees Spirit equally in all."* And the Bible says: "Know ye not that ye are the temple of God, and that the Spirit of God dwelleth in you?"† The Revelation of St. John in the Bible is an allegory of the same principles of yoga cited in the Gita. My Guru sent me to the West especially to show the underlying yoga highway to God to be found in both the Bible and the Bhagavad Gita.

Is there really a God, personal or infinite, that creates and destroys the universe? Has not man in his fear and greed created such a Being after his own image, rather than that a Divine Creator formed man after His image? The presence of so much evil and suffering in the world would seem to support this view.

---

* "He sees truly who perceives the Supreme Lord present equally in all creatures, the Imperishable amidst the perishing" (Bhagavad Gita XIII:27).

† I Corinthians 3:16.

Man's view of the universe is perversely limited by the circumscriptions of his limited mind and senses. Thus he sees created things, but not their essence nor their Creator. In a motion picture, we see the villain and the hero projected on the screen by the same beam of light. The movie villain was created that by contrast we may love and be inspired by the hero. By analyzing the movie, that both the villain and the hero and the events that revolve around them are created by the same principle, we understand that no harm has taken place — everything was a portrayal of shadows and light. The same is true about God's ever-changing motion picture of creation.

Savants who realize their oneness with God see creation as a motion picture of forces emanating from Him. Man, though created in the image of God (a soul that is an individualized part of Him), has become identified with the light-and-shadow relativities of cosmic delusion, or *maya.* When he uses his free choice to adopt those actions by which he frees himself from attachment to *maya,* he understands the true nature of creation and its Creator. In his deluded state, however, man's consciousness of God is limited or expanded according to the greater or lesser degree of his delusion. The man of full realization knows God as ever-existing, ever-conscious, ever-new Bliss; and that all contrasting illusions evolved from this one underlying Cosmic Consciousness.

God created the various kinds of faculties and

potentialities at work in man and in all creation, but man as an individualized part of God endowed with free will becomes engrossed in delusion by misuse of those faculties. In doing so, he himself creates the good or evil role he plays in the cosmic drama, and thereby influences the trend of good or evil events. When man ceases to identify himself with the body and matter, he realizes he is made in the image of God — not before. The enlightened man works with God for the strengthening of good in the world, and for the divine upliftment of others.

* * *

Perhaps you will agree that the world is facing a crisis. What is the cause of it, and what is the remedy?

All nations have to follow the influence of the ascending and descending *yugas.* The present world crisis is due to the upward climb of Dwapara Yuga; in order for the world to become better, evil must be expunged. The forces of evil will cause their own destruction, thus assuring survival of the righteous nations. The conflict between good and evil has been going on since the dawn of history. But as the world is moving upward through the Dwapara Yuga, the electrical or atomic age, there is greater potential not only for good, but also for destruction through the misuse of technology by those who are greedy and desire power. In keeping with the influence of Dwapara Yuga, technology is rapidly moving the general populace to higher levels of achievement. But this progress also creates a greater gap between the achievers and nonachievers. This foments jealousies and social, economic, and political troubles.

Do you think, then, that Communism with its philosophy of equality and its policy of leveling the strata of society to some smooth surface is doing a humanitarian work, and easing God's concern, if you please, about the needs of all His children?

I believe in the brotherhood of man created by mutual love and understanding and cooperation. All worthwhile goals and ennobling ideals should be introduced to the world by spiritual example and good methods, not by brute force and war. Political power without spiritual principles is dangerous. By spiritual principles I do not refer to doctrines of specific religions — which may also be divisive — but to *dharma* or universal principles of righteousness applicable to the well-being of all humanity. To prevent the spread of evil, sometimes righteous war is even necessary. You cannot preach nonviolence and cooperation to a wild tiger, for he will destroy you even before you can expound your philosophy. Some human perpetrators of evil are similarly unresponsive to reason. Any wagers of aggressive war, as was Hitler, will lose. Those who are compelled to fight a righteous war against evil will win. Whether or not a war is righteous is judged by God.

Do you think that America needs to change its character?

America represents the highest in material development, which is much needed in the world; and India represents, through her great masters and prophets, the acme of spiritual realization. In the course of the evolution of civilization, God has brought about these exemplars to show that midway between these two antipodes lies the ideal civilization: a balance between materiality and spirituality. All the world needs to adopt some of the more beautiful aspects of the material progressiveness of America, and also the spiritual idealism of India. America is already embracing a great part of the spiritual civilization of India....India, on the other hand, needs a great deal of the scientific know-how of America to fight disease and poverty and provincialism, which are stains on the name of India's high spiritual heritage. The East should take the best constructive methods of the West, and the West should follow the East's emphasis on God as the supreme goal of life.

Would you like to give a message to the world?

My brothers and sisters of the world: Please remember that God is our Father and He is One. We are all His children, and as such we should adopt constructive means to help each other become physically, mentally, financially, and spiritually ideal citizens of a United States of the World. If in a community of one thousand persons each individual tries by graft, fighting, and chicanery to enrich himself at the expense of others, each person will have nine hundred and ninety-nine enemies; whereas, if each person cooperates with the others — physically, mentally, financially, and spiritually — each one will have nine hundred and ninety-nine friends. If all nations helped one another through love, the whole earth would live in peace with ample opportunity for promoting the well-being of all.

Man seems to forget his spiritual nature and reverts instead to his primal animal instincts. God created man as a potentially spiritual being; so as long as he will give vent to his animal nature, he will have trouble, wars, famine, poverty, and disease. When he will realize the necessity of universal brotherhood, he will create a world of great prosperity and happiness.

It is saddening to see leaders of nations foster untold misery because of greed and hate, instead of getting together in goodwill and harmony to work out their differences. Because of ambitious and evil politicians, the earth has suffered two world wars, and faces the prospect of a third world conflict. If the money spent on destruction were instead collected in an international fund, it could remove the slums of the world, eradicate hunger, and greatly advance medical science, giving every man, woman, and child a better chance to live in the peace of a God-centered life.

History shows that from the dawn of civiliza-

tion hate and selfishness in man have created in-
numerable wars, with their ever-increasing snowball of misery. A third world war would enlarge
this snowball until it would freeze the earth with
misery, poverty, and death. The only way to melt
the snowball of misery is through brotherhood,
love, and divine attunement that comes from God-
uniting methods of meditation. When every soul
will rise above petty divisions in true spiritual understanding, world misery will be consumed in
the fire of the realization of the universality of God
and the brotherhood of man.

Such media as radio and television and air
travel have brought us all together as never before.
We must learn that it can no longer be Asia for Asi-
atics, Europe for Europeans, America for Americans, and so on, but a United States of the World
under God, in which each human being can be an
ideal citizen of the globe with every opportunity
for fulfillment in body, mind, and soul.

That would be my message, my plea, to the
world.

"One World"

Expanding the Boundaries of Our Love and Friendship

By Sri Daya Mata

If we look around us with the eyes of wisdom, it is obvious that world conditions are going to force humankind to develop a closer relationship with God. This globe of the earth, which in past centuries seemed so huge, has comparatively speaking been reduced to the size of an orange. No longer can we think of ourselves as separate from the other peoples and cultures of the world; modern communications and modes of travel have truly brought us all face to face, making it absolutely necessary that we develop the spiritual maturity to understand each other and get along with each other, even as members of the same household must do. Prejudices and small-mindedness — two great weaknesses of human nature — must go.

Extracts from informal talks given at Self-Realization Fellowship International Headquarters, Los Angeles, California

Our guru, Paramahansa Yogananda, foresaw this many decades ago, and spoke of it from his earliest years in this country. I remember in particular the period beginning in the 1940s, when Wendell Willkie wrote the book, *One World.* Paramahansaji very seldom read books, but someone gave this one to him and I had the opportunity to read to him some portions of it. He was extremely impressed. In many of his talks he referred to this ideal of "One World."

Now more than ever we must accept the truth: This *is* one world. It is made up of all different kinds of people with all their multifarious physical appearances, mentalities, interests, motivations. But uniting these endlessly varied blossoms of human individuality there is one basic principle that threads all of us like a garland — and that is God. In His eyes none is greater, none is lesser; we are all His children. God is not the least bit interested in where we were born, which religion we follow, or what the color of our skin is — what does it matter whether our souls wear a red, black, yellow, or white dress? He couldn't care less. But He does care about how we behave. That is the only criterion by which He judges His children. If we are filled with prejudices, we will in like manner reap prejudices. If we are filled with hatred, we will in like manner reap hatred. If we are filled with resentment toward any group of people, it is certain that we are sowing seeds of enmity that one day we ourselves must reap.

Resentment Is Absent
in the Spiritually Mature

To resent anyone because that person is different is childish. Such feelings do not exist in mature, divine souls. Prejudicial minds resent people who are Democrats; or resent people who are Republicans; or resent people who are members of this race or that religion — why? Because they insist on the viewpoint of the little "I" or ego. Its self-interest is childishly small and petty. Have you ever watched children playing together? They can be having the time of their lives — laughing, joking, sharing their toys — then suddenly one picks up something the other child wants, and before you know it they are fighting. One is hitting the other over the head and the other is screaming, and you have a real battle going on! Too many "adults" behave exactly like this — look at the number of wars going on in so many nations around the world. These are the reactions born of the immature development of the perpetrators. The mature individual understands and accepts that there are many different viewpoints in this world, and that none is exclusively right.

The message the Lord is trying to convey to humanity today, through all of His teachers, is this: We must enlarge our vision and do away with the boundaries of prejudices; they can no longer exist in the era of the new world that is being born.

How different the Hindu thinks the Christian

is, and how different the Christian thinks the
Hindu is. The wonderful trend of this age, as our
Guru predicted, is that more and more the West is
valuing India's system of yoga and meditation, and
more and more India — primarily through teachers
like Paramahansa Yogananda and teachings such as
ours — is learning to appreciate the true meaning
of Christ and his universal message.

NOT COMPETING RELIGIONS,
BUT UNIVERSAL TRUTH

To fight over religion is nonsense. No religion
has a monopoly on God; they all reflect a particular facet of Truth. We should therefore respect the
God in them all. That is one of the basic principles
of the message Paramahansa Yogananda brought to
the West, sent by his Gurus: Man should think in
terms not of competing religions, but of one Truth,
which like a sparkling diamond has many, many
facets, each reflecting variously God's light.

Underlying the varied beliefs and practices,
there are spiritual concepts common to all religions. . . . Paramahansaji tried always to draw the attention of devotees to these universal, fundamental truths — not merely as a matter of belief and
dissertation, but as a practical necessity to be practiced in their daily lives. The most important of
these — taught by the saviors of mankind throughout the ages — is for each individual to have direct,
personal communion with the Divine. This is in-

deed sorely needed. It is the reason for which, as our Guru said many times, Mahavatar Babaji in communion with Christ sent this message to the world at this time. We do not need more religions; what we need are people who exemplify the spirituality of religion.

The problem with religion today (and this applies equally to Christianity, Hinduism, and all others) is that people have become lost in dogmas and external modes of worship. It is not enough to go to church or to the temple and hear the minister or priest quote scripture — "We ought not to have prejudice; we ought to accept all as our brothers; we ought to be loving and forgiving" — and then go back to our homes and quarrel with our husbands, wives, or neighbors; or discriminate against one another. Words alone cannot make people accept one another, any more than can hitting them over the head with sticks! No amount of trying to force people to come together is going to unite them. They need to be shown how to uncover their real nature — a discovery made only through meditation and communion with God.

By meditation you gradually slough off the erroneous perception that you are a finite little body, caged in a limited portion of space, pulled this way and that by moods, prejudices, hatreds, resentments, envies, desires for material things. You realize: "I am not that! Why should I continue to burden myself with these petty feelings and cravings, when the whole kingdom of Heaven is mine?"

The more we strive by daily meditation to dwell in that consciousness, to remember our real nature, the more we will express that divinity which was in Christ and is in every one of us. This is the message of Self-Realization. It is a message that India can accept, that Christians can accept, that all religionists can accept. It does not go against the teaching of any faith.

Paramahansa Yogananda's
predictions on...

THE FUTURE OF SECTARIAN RELIGION

From lectures given on August 22, 1933 and August 27, 1939:

Every church does good, and for that I love them all. They will truly fulfill their high calling when they become places of God-communion. They should be like hives, filled with the honey of God-realization. Unless this truth becomes more manifest in religion, you will see that the church as such will gradually disappear....

The dissatisfaction of real truth-seekers with dogmatism, and the emptiness of organization without individual Self-realization, will force a great world change in the concept of religion.

***

From a lecture given on May 21, 1944:

The world's various religions are based more or

It is something all peoples must accept — or this world will go through such chaos as you cannot believe. The Lord is determined that man shall be more loving and understanding. If we don't do so willingly, then we shall have to learn the hard way. One way or the other, mankind's attitude is destined to change. We have to become more aware of God in our lives. And we shall. But let us

less on the *beliefs* of man. But the true basis of religion should be a science that all devotees may apply in order to reach our one Father-God. Yoga is that science. The practice of a *science of religion* is imperative. Different dogmatic "isms" have kept mankind divided, although Jesus pointed out: "If a house be divided against itself, that house cannot stand" (Mark 3:25). Unity among various religions may be brought about only when the individuals who practice those religions become actually aware of God within. Then we shall have a true brotherhood of man under the Fatherhood of God.

***

We should begin to build world unity with the idea that has been initiated by Self-Realization Fellowship: a "Church of All Religions"; not eclecticism, but respect for all religions as constituting various paths to God. Such temples, dedicated to the one God that all religions worship, should be built everywhere. I predict that this will come about.

not wait for heartache and suffering and struggle; let us do it willingly. How? By meditation — developing a personal, loving communion with God — and by practicing in our daily lives the basic spiritual and moral principles given down the centuries by the great saints and sages.

CEASE BEING PREOCCUPIED WITH "ME" AND "MINE"

One such principle is this: Forget the lower self by seeking the higher Self. What does this mean? Cease being so preoccupied with "me," "I," "mine," and begin to think in terms of doing good to others — including others in our circle of friendship, our circle of brotherhood, our circle of love. Paramahansaji often quoted: "Love and I drew a circle, and drew the whole world in." What a beautiful thought this is!

You may well say, "It is impossible for me to love all people." All right, then start with a smaller goal. Begin in the environment where God has placed you. Express your love for the members of your own family by making a greater effort to understand and be patient with them, rather than fighting with them. Don't be a "street angel and a house devil." Such persons behave like saints outside the home, speaking piously with folded hands; but when they get back amongst their family members, they let them have it! This is wrong; what we profess in words, we should do our best to live. We may not immediately be able to do it one hundred percent, but we have to start somewhere. We must learn to manifest in our daily behavior the Christ principle, the Love principle, which is within us. There is no better place to start than with those whom God has drawn to cross our path — our family and the others with whom we associate each day.

So, to forget self by seeking the higher Self means to look always to the good in people as well as to the good in yourself. Recognize and bring out the qualities of the higher Self — the divine qualities of the soul that reside within you and within everyone else.

BE A HUMBLE GIVER

Scripture also teaches us to give rather than take in life. Isn't that a beautiful ideal? Be a giver, not a taker — materially, spiritually, morally, or in any other way. Of course, it is good to know how to receive graciously; this in itself can be a gift we offer the giver! But learn primarily to give of yourself — of your heart, of your understanding. Give of anything you have, but give. It is a very broadening experience, which takes you beyond thinking only of your little self. How essential this is. The self-circumscribed ego is the source of all of your problems; analyze it and you will find it to be so.

In doing good to others, avoid the egotistical pitfall of spiritual self-satisfaction. Give humbly with no expectation of reward.

In my early days in the ashram, someone wrote to Paramahansaji a sweet note that deeply impressed my soul. It was a devotional thought by some saint, and it was signed: "Less than the dust." I can't tell you how that inspired me — what a sublime, thrilling ideal that is to me: to live in that perfect humility wherein one never thinks highly of himself.

Now, I don't mean that one should indulge in the false piety of an inferiority complex. We can never be "inferior"; we are God's children. True humility is the realization: "Lord, You are the Light; I am only the bulb." When the light is gone from the bulb, it is worth little; but when that illumining power is present, the bulb brightens the darkness in the world. So it is with each one of us, when the Divine Light shows though the bulb of our consciousness. Everyone dreams of doing some good in this world; that is not wrong — we *should* want to. But always remember, "Of myself, Lord, I can do nothing." Convince yourself of that; for anything that increases the ego builds a barrier between you and God.

Those barriers between man and God must be removed if this world is to know greater harmony and peace. Usually people consider the cause of wars and international strife in terms of politics or diplomatic relations. We need to look deeper. Our Guru told us: "The world will continue to have warfare and natural calamities until all people correct their wrong thoughts and behavior. Wars are brought about...by widespread material selfishness. Banish selfishness — individual, industrial, political, national — and you will have no more wars."

The whole purpose of self-discipline — of living by these principles we have discussed — is to remove those ego-barriers, selfishness, in whatever form they exist. Though many in the modern world believe that self-discipline is unnecessary, a relic of Puritanism, it is completely unrealistic to think that one can find happiness and peace of mind by merely doing as he pleases. It cannot be. Many unhappy and confused people today are the result of overleniency on the part of parents who said, "I didn't have anything when I was a child; I want my child to have everything." Indulgence does the child a great disservice. Such parents may give their children a material abundance, but neglect what the child really needs: kindness, love, understanding, communication, and the discipline to develop into emotionally and spiritually mature individuals.

Paramahansaji often reminded us: "To give food to the hungry is good; to give knowledge and mental strength to the weak and ignorant is better, in order that they can help themselves; but to give God to the souls of others — to rouse in them a love and yearning for God, and to point out the path that leads to Him — this is the greatest form of service one can render." God and God alone is the answer to man's search, his struggle for happiness and fulfillment. Without God there is no hope for man; but with Him, each individual life becomes successful in the highest way, and the world at large begins to experience peace.

WILL WORLD PEACE EVER COME ON EARTH?

Someone asked me recently, "Did Paramahansaji predict that peace will ever reign on earth?" No, he did not. This is not a realistic expectation. This world was not intended to be a place of unalloyed contentment. Yes, there will be periods in the history of this earth when peace will be more predominant than at other times; there is no question about that. But it is not realistic to dream of utopia in this material world, because God did not create it for that purpose. The kingdom of heaven is within, as Christ told us. Having forsaken that kingdom, man becomes a whining, weak, naughty, angry, sensuous, struggling creature, incarnating in this world again and again until he comprehends the one purpose of this earthly schoolhouse: to prod us to reclaim that divine kingdom within. As long as man exists in this imperfect external world, he will go through turmoil and struggle to one degree or another.

"Well," you will say, "then there is no use making an effort to improve the situation." But this is missing the point. The earth is a school where we come to learn how to behave — that's all it is. It is easy to behave nobly toward those who love us, but how do we react toward those who hate and revile us? Can we respond with love, understanding, forgiveness, in all situations, and under all conditions? If we keep that ideal before us, and strive always to behave in the highest possible way, we will know for certain that we are progressing spiritually, that every circumstance we face in this life is drawing us closer to God. To know Him is to have the inward awareness of heavenly bliss no matter what may befall us outwardly. That is the testimony offered by the lives of Jesus Christ and of all the great ones.

It is practice of these basic principles of truth and right behavior — plus meditation on God — that gradually transforms the totality of man's character. We must not expect that we can become Christs overnight; that is not what is asked of us. All we need do is strive each day to express a little more of that love, that positive-mindedness, that cheerfulness, that undaunted courage which are of God's presence in our souls. Be a carrier of sunshine, a carrier of goodwill. Each and every one of us has that divine spark within. It rests with us to bring it out — for our own highest benefit, and that of our world.

YOGA: THE SCIENCE OF RELIGION

BY BROTHER ANANDAMOY

L ast year while in India for the celebrations of the birth centennial of Paramahansa Yogananda, I was interviewed on the national television network, and one question asked was, "Considering all the problems in the world today, shouldn't we concentrate on solving them instead of talking about religion?"

I am sure many people have entertained that same question in connection with this Parliament of the World's Religions. Of course, it is necessary to address those troubling issues. But if you analyze deeply enough, you come to the conclusion that the root cause of the world's problems is that humanity has turned its back on God and the laws of God — which include the laws of nature. Whether we are talking about social, political, economic, or ecological problems — at the level of the individual, the family, the nation, or the world — the only solution that will be lastingly effective is for humanity

Extracts from a talk given at Parliament of the World's Religions, Chicago, September 3, 1993

to turn back to God, back to *dharma,* the eternal laws of righteousness that uphold the universal structure and the very existence of human beings. When there is harmony with the divine workings of creation, problems will solve themselves. It is as simple as that — and as difficult as that.

Consider the spiritual confusion that characterizes our modern era. When Paramahansa Yogananda came to America in 1920, the focal point of his first lecture here was "What is the purpose of life?"* It is interesting, because even today, in spite of all the scientific and technological advancements, people in general still do not know what life is really all about. And what is amazing is that they don't even ask. Most people are so caught up in the external procedures and processes of life that it doesn't occur to them to entertain such questions as "Why am I here?" And most of those who do inquire arrive at a wrong answer.

Not long ago, there was a popular radio program in Los Angeles, hosted by a clinical psychologist. After a short talk about some aspect of psychology, people could call in with questions about their personal problems. I listened one time when a woman called in and asked, "Would you please help me? I'm so confused. Can you tell me, what is the meaning of life?" The answer given by that psychologist was: "Life has no meaning." The gist of the reply was this: Life gives you opportunities —

* In Boston on October 6, 1920, as a delegate to the International Congress of Religious Liberals.

opportunities to have relationships, to work, to make money. With the money you can buy all sorts of things, and you can have all kinds of pleasures. But, emphatically, life itself has no meaning.

This viewpoint is not at all uncommon today. A professor of psychology at the University of Massachusetts, Susan Whitbourne, conducted extensive research, starting back in the 1960s and continuing to the present, analyzing what Americans do, how they feel, and so on. (And from what I have observed, her findings are true also in Europe and elsewhere in the world where the consumer ethic is taking root.) She found that people "have lost a sense of personal meaning. They are working more, but are far more full of despair." Why? They are desperately seeking fulfillment, and never finding it.

She tested and retested people throughout these years, and found "a steep decline in integrity, a personality factor that relates to wholeness, honesty, and meaning in life." At first she thought this condition applied only to people whose lifestyle revolves around acquiring wealth and possessions. But she found the same symptoms in all groups of society, and she concluded that this reflects "a general, society-wide crisis of morality and purpose, affecting adults of all ages. The scores on life-satisfaction are so low, they couldn't go any lower."

That is why the world is in such a mess today: People do not know what the purpose of life is. As a result, their ambitions and behavior are guided

by values that are out of harmony with truth, and
are therefore destructive to personal and planetary
well-being. The world will not change unless this
situation is turned around.

WHAT IS THE PURPOSE OF LIFE?

What *is* the purpose of life? Paramahansa Yogananda explained it very clearly. His explanation
was not new or revolutionary; it has been in the
scriptures of the world's great religions for millen-
nia. But much is hidden in symbolism or allegory.
Part of Paramahansa Yogananda's mission was to
winnow out the truth and explain it in simple,
modern language so that we can understand it—
and not only understand it, but put it into practice.

He pointed out that, superficially, human beings
are all different—in their psychological and emotional makeup, in the roles they play in life, their
jobs, their desires. But underneath those differences there are two things that every human being,
without exception, wants and *needs.* One is freedom from all forms of suffering and want; and the
other is infinite happiness—an absolute fulfillment
that includes perfect peace, love, wisdom, joy.

Essentially, what we are seeking is God, whether
or not we use that name. Paramahansa Yogananda
said: "God-consciousness is bliss-consciousness." We
will never feel satisfied until we have that perfect
happiness and complete fulfillment; this is a fundamental key to understanding the human condition.

But where is humanity seeking it? In the things of the world: in possessions, in outer conditions, in relationships with other persons. It is mathematically impossible to find that perfection in anything or anyone or any condition in this world, owing to the very nature of creation.

Creation is built on the principle of duality. You cannot have a picture with only one color; you have to have contrast. Likewise, there could be no manifestation of creation without duality. But look at the desires that motivate human beings: Each of us would like to have just the good things—the pleasant, the beautiful, the positive—and not have to deal with all the trash and unpleasantness. That is impossible. In this dualistic world, there cannot be pleasure without pain, light without darkness, good without evil, life without death. You cannot have one side of the coin without the other. It comes down to that basic principle: What we crave at the deepest level of our being cannot be found in anything the world can give us.

One of the ancient scriptures of India says, in relation to this truth: "Know it now or after a thousand incarnations." In other words, do you want to go on seeking in the wrong place and continually be frustrated? This is exactly what that professor of psychology found: "They are working more, but are far more full of despair." People are frantically searching, but they cannot find what they are looking for; and that leads to despair. And not just despair; tremendous resentment and anger accrue in the process — a lot of anger, a lot of violence. Again, it is because people are seeking in the wrong place and therefore not finding true fulfillment.

This may seem a rather pessimistic picture of life. It isn't really, if we understand the divine rationale behind God's universal plan. He wants us to be reunited with Him, so He arranged the cosmic scheme to prevent our becoming satisfied with anything less. In attaining union with God, we fulfill the purpose of our existence.

Where Can God Be Found?

So, the next question is where do we find God? God, or Spirit, or the Infinite Consciousness (it doesn't matter what word you want to use) is all-pervading, omnipresent. But as long as we are looking for That outside of ourselves, we are using the senses and the mortal mind, the faculties through which we cognize the outer world. Great saints of all religions have affirmed this truth: the senses and the human intellect cannot perceive God; these gross instruments are far too limited. We have to go inside. There, through the intuition of the soul, we find Him.

On this point, the esoteric teachings of all the great religions agree: what we seek is inside. Interiorization is a fundamental step in the science of yoga. Jesus Christ said, "The kingdom of God is within you." St. Teresa of Avila wrote to her nuns, "Remember what St. Augustine said. He had been searching for God everywhere and finally found Him within himself. It is most important that you understand this truth, that God is within."

Paramahansa Yogananda explained that because the human intellect is too limited to answer the basic questions—Who am I? What is behind this creation? Who is its creator?—ancient India's *rishis,* enlightened sages, evolved yoga as the technique of spiritual inquiry.

Yoga is taught not only in India, of course; it is really the esoteric essence of all the great religions. St. Teresa of Avila wrote about the different stages of prayer—oral prayer, mental prayer, prayer of recollection, prayer of quiet, prayer of communion, prayer of union. This is yoga in Christian terminology, a description of the successive stages of interiorization. In the inner stillness, there comes the awareness of God within oneself (prayer of communion) and then the uniting of one's consciousness with Him (prayer of union).

She also used a very interesting illustration. She said that just as a turtle withdraws its legs into the shell, so we have to interiorize—withdraw our consciousness from the outer faculties—in order to find God. What is interesting is that Lord Krishna in the Bhagavad Gita used that same illustration of the turtle.* Krishna lived centuries be-

---

* "When the yogi, like a tortoise withdrawing its limbs, can fully retire his senses from the objects of perception, his wisdom manifests steadiness" (Bhagavad Gita II:58). (From Paramahansa Yogananda's translation and commentary, *God Talks With Arjuna: The Bhagavad Gita,* published by Self-Realization Fellowship.)

fore Christ; St. Teresa in the sixteenth century—
and at that time the Gita had not yet been trans-
lated into Western languages. Truth is the same in
every age.

Another example comes from a Christian monk,
Jean de Saint-Samson, one of the great reformers of
the Carmelite order in the seventeenth century. He
said, "The faculties are there in an arrested condition. All is fixed upon God. All is merged." That is
an exact description of the process of yoga.* This
man knew what he was talking about, but he did
not say how to do it. Neither did St. Teresa. Even
Patanjali, the great master who wrote the *Yoga Sutras,* gave all the principles, and the definition of
yoga: neutralization of the alternating waves in
consciousness, which leads to union with God. But
how to do it? He did not say; he did not give a technique. The same truth is in the Old Testament: "Be
still, and know that I am God." But the Bible, too,
does not say how to do it. Lord Krishna personally
taught the highest techniques of yoga to his disciples, yet those methods were not set forth in his
discourse in the Bhagavad Gita.

So the next point is: How to go within? That is
what Paramahansa Yogananda has given to us: the
definite science of attaining direct, personal experience of God.

---

* Reference to the last four of the eight steps of uniting the consciousness with God, as outlined by the sage Patanjali, foremost ancient exponent of Yoga. Patanjali's eightfold path of Yoga is explained on pages
159–60.

The Scientific Key to Experience of God

That science is embodied in the techniques of Kriya Yoga. The basic key to Kriya practice, which was lost for centuries, is an understanding of energy. In the Dark Ages, man had lost the knowledge of the subtle forces and energies in creation — electricity, magnetism, and so on. Now, through material science, we are again familiar with the concept of energy. We work with electricity, for example — turning it on, turning it off, as we please. And we can also understand the scientific principle that all our organs and faculties — the brain, the heart, the senses — are operated by energy. The Sanskrit word for it is *prana,* the force that sustains life in the body.

In ordinary waking consciousness, that life energy flows down from the brain through the spine and nervous system and out into the muscles, organs, and senses. This produces in our consciousness a powerful identification with the physical body; and, through the senses, with the physical world. However, since realization of God is impossible through the senses, we need to learn how to withdraw the energy from the senses and direct it inward to awaken the higher spiritual faculties of divine perception, which are dormant in the subtle centers of consciousness *(chakras)* in the spine and brain.

That is the basic principle of Raja Yoga. Paramahansa Yogananda said, "Where the energy is, there is the consciousness." In other words, learn to withdraw that energy from externals and concentrate it within, where God is waiting for you. Perception of God is as simple as that, in principle: it is made possible by energy-control, or *pranayama*.

As I mentioned, this understanding had been lost for centuries. Even in India today most people still think that *pranayama* refers to breathing exercises. It is much deeper than that. It means control, mastery *(yama)*, over the energy *(prana)*. This science is mentioned, however obliquely, in many of the scriptures of the world religions. What is the greatest commandment in the Bible, in both the Old and New Testaments? "Love God with all your heart, all your mind, all your soul, all your strength." That commandment gives in one sentence the whole essence of Raja Yoga, of Kriya Yoga. Strength means energy. The mind, the feeling, the energy — all need to be directed inward, so that the consciousness is completely absorbed in God.

In Yoga this state of union with God is called *samadhi,* which literally means "to direct together" — to direct together the faculties and lead the awareness inside, where God is. Religion is based on this high principle of communion with God, leading to union with God. Many of the rituals practiced in the different faiths symbolize exactly that.

For example, the holy communion of Christianity — eating the bread, drinking the wine, the "flesh and blood of Christ"—is an outer symbol of the inner process of God-communion: uniting, or merging with, the cosmic vibration of *Aum,* the Holy Ghost (the essential vibratory substance of which the universe consists), and with the Christ Consciousness.*

Another example is the fire ceremony common in India, in which clarified butter is poured into a consecrated fire. Again, this is an exoteric representation of an esoteric process: purifying our little human consciousness and uniting it with the Infinite. The true meaning of these symbolic rituals is little understood.

In his *Autobiography of a Yogi,* Paramahansa Yogananda quoted one of India's great philosophers and masters, Swami Shankara: "Outward ritual cannot destroy ignorance, because they are not mutually contradictory." Ignorance means body consciousness, sensory consciousness, mortal consciousness—that which keeps us unaware of our true divine nature. He went on: "Realized knowledge alone"—meaning actual *experience* of truth —"destroys ignorance."

---

* When Spirit manifests creation, It becomes the Trinity: Father, Son, Holy Ghost, or *Sat, Tat, Aum*. The Father *(Sat),* or Cosmic Consciousness, is God as the Creator existing beyond creation. The Holy Ghost *(Aum)* is the vibratory power of God that objectifies or becomes creation. Immanent in the *Aum* is the Son *(Tat),* or Christ Consciousness, God's intelligence omnipresent in creation. It is the universal consciousness, oneness with God, manifested by Jesus, Krishna, and other avatars. Great saints and yogis know it as the state of *samadhi* meditation wherein their consciousness has become identified with the intelligence in every particle of creation; they feel the entire universe as their own body.

That is why Paramahansa Yogananda said, "I do not give you rituals; I give you techniques that will enable you actually to experience that which rituals only symbolize."

In bringing the Self-Realization Fellowship techniques of meditation to the world, Paramahansa Yogananda also brought the means for realizing the oneness of the religions. In communion with God there can be no divisiveness between one religion and another, because there is only one God. Externally, of course, the various world religions do have differences. They were introduced at different times, to meet the specific needs and understanding of people in those ages; therefore, they teach different dogmas, approaches, ceremonies, and so forth. But the esoteric core — which most people do not even know is there — is the same: communion with God within, and ultimate union with Him....

Yoga, being the science of religion, focuses on the esoteric truth underlying exoteric practices and beliefs. What are some of these outer religious practices? Going to a church or temple; listening to a sermon or to recitation of scriptures; singing of hymns; watching a religious ritual or ceremony; perhaps telling stories of religious figures —Krishna, Rama, Buddha, Jesus — or stories about historical events, such as how God led the Jews through the desert, and so on. In East and West, it is the same. In all of these practices, where is the mind? It is directed outward — to some outer activity.

This is true also of some of the forms of mental

worship practiced by various religions. In Christianity, for example, there is the practice of mentally visualizing an episode in the life of Jesus, such as his birth or crucifixion (this is termed "meditation" in that tradition). In other religions, including those of India, there are similar practices: mentally visualizing a whole drama, or watching an elaborate ceremonial worship of the deity. Again, where are the mind and attention? They are directed to outer events.

I am not saying these practices are wrong; on the contrary, they are a necessary phase of spiritual growth. People need to learn to think about spiritual things, even if only for a brief time once a week, instead of being totally absorbed in material pursuits and thoughts. But these outer practices are only the first phase.

The deeper practice of religion consists of going into the inner stillness, perceiving God manifested within — as peace, light, *Aum,* joy, love, and so on — and then becoming one with That. This is called "contemplation" in Christian terminology, "meditation" in the terminology of the science of yoga.

Over the centuries during which this higher knowledge of yoga was lost, very few have been able to achieve this state. St. Teresa's nuns belonged to a contemplative order, but she wrote that only a few of them could go into that perfectly absorbed state of consciousness. The others remained on the level of oral and mental prayer. Of course, out of the masses there have been exceptions — persons who

had developed such profound, overwhelming devotion that when they saw, for example, a statue or
painting that represented God, they lost all outer
consciousness and were absorbed in *samadhi*. But
most of us do not possess that devotional intensity;
that is why we need yoga techniques.

Paramahansa Yogananda came with a special
dispensation to make known to the world the ancient techniques of yoga from the higher ages. In
addition to the highest techniques of Kriya Yoga,
he also taught several other techniques that are
preparatory and auxiliary to Kriya, and are in themselves very effective methods of divine communion, including the *Aum* technique of meditation
and the Hong-Sau technique of concentration.*

Not long ago we received a letter at our Self-
Realization Fellowship International Headquarters
in Los Angeles from a fourteen-year-old girl, who at
the time had learned only the Hong-Sau technique.
"First of all," she wrote, "the Hong-Sau technique is
the best thing that I ever learned, because it affects
and changes my whole life. After I practice the
technique, then mentally, physically, emotionally,
and spiritually I feel peaceful. It is not a normal, human, describable calm. It is the ultimate, peaceful
calm. No words can describe it." That is the peace
which "passeth all understanding," which is an aspect of God. She goes on, "Emotionally, I have
much more inner happiness, and I am much more

* Paramahansa Yogananda's instruction on these techniques is given in a
series of lessons for home study, available from Self-Realization Fellowship.

tolerant, I am much kinder, much more giving."
Meditation is not, as some people think, a selfish
endeavor. It lifts and expands the consciousness,
making it natural to think of other people.

Then she writes, "It is as if my soul speaks after I practice this technique. When I close my eyes
and gaze at the third eye,* God's big bright white
light is gazing back at me. Overall, I feel a great
peace, which in no other way can be expressed
except in itself. Thank you for allowing me to receive this beautiful technique."

How Yoga Meditation Leads
to God-Awareness

The techniques take you inside. But that is not
the end. In fact, it is *after* practice of the techniques
that actual meditation begins. Some people think,
"Well, I've practiced the techniques; now I can stop
meditating and get on with something else." No.
That is missing the point. You have made the effort
to go within, into "the kingdom of God within you."
Now, let your consciousness become absorbed in
the presence of God, in the awareness of God.

That is what real meditation consists of — communion with God — not psychic experiences or
phenomena, as some people are inclined to think.
"The path to God is not a circus," Paramahansa

---

* The single eye referred to by Jesus: "When thine eye is single, thy
whole body also is full of light....Take heed therefore that the light
which is in thee be not darkness" (Luke 11:34-35).

Yogananda said. It requires self-forgetfulness; not thinking "what am I going to get"—wanting visions or phenomenal displays.

The experiences that come in real meditation are of God's essential aspects—peace, light, *Aum,* joy. When in meditation you perceive any of those manifestations, realize that this is God; give yourself into that. Paramahansa Yogananda said it perfectly, "Just lose yourself in love for God."

There is another point I want to make very

Paramahansa Yogananda's predictions on...

THE FUTURE OF YOGA

From a lecture in 1934:

There will come a day, after I have left this physical form, when there will be a great surge of spiritual enthusiasm and interest in God. The message of India, the spiritual leader of the world, will sweep the earth.

***

From a lecture given on February 16, 1941:

The science of yoga will take hold in this country more than any other form of spiritual seeking. The entire trend will be away from churches, where people go only to hear a sermon, and into schools and quiet places where they will go to meditate and really find God.

strongly because often it is not understood. Many people practice meditation with an attitude of trying to force an experience of God, straining for results. The experience or perception of God will never come through force — never. It comes through surrender. It comes through purity, through sincerity, through giving; and then through leaving it up to God to decide when to give you what you want. That is why Jesus said, "The pure in heart shall see God." What does purity mean? Selfishness is gone; in your consciousness there is just One: God. If you think of self — "what *I* want," "what God should be giving to *me*" — you are not meditating. Meditation means concentration on God to the exclusion of everything else. The self, the ego, has to get out to make room for God. In meditation there is a total self-abandonment to the One: "You, my God."

Another important point to understand about meditation is that sometimes nothing happens — one feels no peace, no sense of the Divine Presence, nothing. Then the tendency is to say, "Well, I'm not getting anything from my meditations. It's useless. I'm not worthy of God's response." Nothing could be further from the truth. Every saint has gone through periods when God didn't seem to respond.

Sri Gyanamata, one of the great disciples of Paramahansa Yogananda, said, "Do not mind His silence. Remember, He is listening." She also said that her goal was to love as God loves, as His saints love, without asking anything in return. When you persist in meditation, even when you experience nothing, then you are learning to make your love unconditional.

Carrying the Consciousness of God's Presence Into Daily Life

Meditation is the foundation of the spiritual life. But there is another aspect also. Obviously, we cannot meditate all the time; we have our work to do, our outer role to play. This too is a part of spiritual discipline. Paramahansa Yogananda said, "Our spiritual and material duties should work together like two stallions, pulling the car of life harmoniously and uniformly to one happy goal."

"All outer duties should be spiritualized," he said. That is, everything should be done with the consciousness of God within.

Outer works and their results in themselves can never give us complete satisfaction and fulfillment. Let me give an example. I came to America to study under Frank Lloyd Wright. He was considered the king of architecture at that time, a man of great fame and genius. He knew he was a genius; yet he was not happy. One day I was present when he expressed some of the deep inner frustration he felt, and I saw that inwardly he was still unfulfilled. Like so many, he was seeking happiness and fulfillment in the wrong place — in his case, through fame and through his creative ability.

By way of contrast, when I was in Italy I had

seen the paintings of Fra Angelico, a famous painter of the fifteenth century and a deeply spiritual man. It is said that as he painted his portraits of Christ and the Madonna and the saints, tears of devotion streamed down his face. He didn't paint in order to have satisfaction through fame or through creativity. He found that satisfaction through his inner communion with God. And his act of painting was an offering to God.

The point is not that we have to cry in devotion to God when we work, but that our actions should be an offering to the Divine. Then our work is spiritualized. It doesn't matter what our occupation is; God isn't concerned about that. The saints of the various religions have been householders and monastics; they have worked in all occupations; they have been on all rungs of the social ladder. It was not their outer role that made them saints; it was their inner consciousness.

So while you are working, once in a while stop for a moment and inwardly say to God, "I do this for You." Then you become God-centered, even in the midst of outer activities.

REAWAKENING OUR DIVINE NATURE

There is a story in Greek mythology of Theseus, a great king and hero of Athens, who went down to the netherworld. The lord of the netherworld offered him a chair. Theseus didn't realize it was the chair of forgetfulness, and he sat down. Instantly he

forgot everything — who he was, where he came
from, why he came down to the netherworld in the
first place. He just sat there, until Heracles came
and got him out. That story is an allegory. It's about
man, and woman. We came down to this material
plane, and we have forgotten where we came from,
we have forgotten what we are, and we have forgotten why we are here. So we have to listen to the
saints. They all say the same thing, essentially: We
are children of God, and we have to reawaken our
divine nature.

Never forget that. The world will say, "No, you
are just a mortal human being." They teach in
school that man is a rational animal. So people behave accordingly. They forget: We are children of
God. Our true essence is the soul: made in the image of God — immortal, indestructible, ever-blissful
Infinite Consciousness.

As Paramahansa Yogananda often said, if you
have a lump of gold and you cover it with mud are
you going to claim it's no longer gold? Of course
not; it is still gold. "We are and ever have been the
children of God," he said. "We are like gold in the
mud: when the mud of ignorance is cleansed away,
the shining gold of the soul, made in God's image,
is seen within."

That is the purpose of religion — indeed, the
purpose of life — to wash off the mud of ignorance, so we can know who we really are. And it
is the answer to the problems we face in the
world. Can you imagine what this world would be

like if it were filled with people who had found within themselves the great love and joy and peace and wisdom of God?

So every day give some time to God, give some time to meditation. Remember and affirm who you really are — a child of God — and share your innate goodness with others; and you will be a happy person, contributing to a better world.

God bless you all.

PART IV
THE NEW WORLD

A World Without Boundaries

Is Peace Possible in Today's World?

Change Yourself, Transform the World

If you contact God within yourself, you will know that He is in everyone, that He has become the children of all races. Then you cannot be an enemy to anyone. If the whole world could love with that universal love, there would be no need for men to arm themselves against one another. By our own Christlike example we must bring unity among all religions, all nations, all races.

—Paramahansa Yogananda
in Man's Eternal Quest

A World Without Boundaries

By Paramahansa Yogananda

Wherever different minds meet in the spirit of fellowship, there we find a great harmony, peace, happiness, understanding, and cooperation in life's activities. With so many troubles plaguing this earth of ours...never before was there a greater necessity for peace than now.

I believe there will always be wars, until perchance we all become so spiritual that by the evolution of our individual natures we will make war unnecessary. No matter what their differences, if great minds such as Jesus, Krishna, Buddha, Mohammed, sat together, they would never use the engines of science to try to destroy each other. Where there is understanding, peace reigns. Why must people feel it necessary to fight? The power of guns evokes no wisdom, nor has it ever accomplished lasting peace.

Extracts from a talk given in Los Angeles, California, February 26, 1939. The complete talk is published in The Divine Romance (Collected Talks and Essays, Volume II) *by Paramahansa Yogananda (Los Angeles: Self-Realization Fellowship).*

War is like poison in the system. When we have toxins in our body, that impurity has to get out somehow. So we suffer from disease. Likewise, when there is too much selfishness in the international system, that poison breaks out in the world as the disease of war. Many people are killed, and then for a little while there is a lull. But war comes again — and will come again and again — so long as there will be ignorance, and so long as the individual man has not become a perfect citizen of the world.

God gave us intelligence, and He placed us in

Paramahansa Yogananda's predictions on...

IS THERE A WAY TO PREVENT
ANOTHER WORLD WAR?

From Autobiography of a Yogi, *published in 1946:*

Consulting history, one may reasonably state that man's problems have not been solved by the use of brute force. World War I produced an earth-chilling snowball of dread karma that swelled into World War II. Only the warmth of brotherhood can melt the present colossal snowball of sanguinary karma that may otherwise grow into World War III.

From a lecture in 1948:

This is the time to preach brotherhood. No matter how dark you think the picture is, do not be too an environment where we must use that intelligence. The universe is like a shell, and we are like little chicks moving about within it. But what is beyond this shell of matter?...

We should use our intelligence to analyze the mysteries of life and to explore the secrets the Heavenly Father has hidden behind nature. How much better use of intelligence this would be, than the creation of bigger and more destructive instruments of war. We must use our intelligence to have peace among ourselves....

---

discouraged. I know there is a God who gives to the nations of the world what is for their good. They reap good or bad results according to their karma....

This is a time when God is bumping the heads of Communism, Imperialism, Capitalism — all isms that believe in the power of force. I make one prediction now: *The world is not going down to destruction.* So don't be frightened. Believe in your Father. He will protect you if you remember His ideals, if you keep faith in Him. We are moving upward. The twelve hundred years of the material cycle have passed, and three hundred of the twenty-four hundred years of the atomic age are gone. Then there will be the mental and the spiritual ages. We are not going down. No matter what happens, the Spirit will win. I predict this; and that America's democracy and practical material power combined with India's spiritual power will prevail and conquer the world.

LOVE THE WORLD AS YOU LOVE
YOUR NATION AND FAMILY

International understanding is much clouded by lack of realization that individual happiness is included in family happiness, family happiness in community happiness, community happiness in national happiness, and national happiness in international happiness.

Love of family is inherently strong. Through family love, God became the father to love you through wisdom, and He became the mother because He wanted to give you unconditional love. God became the lover and the beloved to unite souls in an expanded love. He became the friend to unite souls in a pure, impersonal love that makes no demands. In friendship there is no compulsion; it comes through the choice of the heart. Such friendship should exist between husband and wife, child and parent, in all human relations. Friendship is a great factor in bringing peace in the international family of the world.

No one can love his nation without learning the first lesson in love, which is to love his family. The baby's initial cries are for milk, but soon it invests its love in the mother and father. Then, as it grows older, it learns to love its country. When that soul becomes Christlike, it begins to love the world.

You are a member of the worldwide human race. Don't forget it. You must love the world as you love your nation and your family. This is difficult to learn, but the task of Self-Realization Fellowship is to show you how. We teach that it is by fellowship with God that fellowship with man must be established; because only when you know God and see Him in all can you love the Jew and Christian, Muslim and Hindu, with the same spirit. I was taught this as a child, but it was more or less a forced intellectual concept. It wasn't an understanding from within. I tried to love the whole world, but it was not easy. As soon as I looked at my family, my love lost itself there. But one by one, many of those dearest to me died. I thought that nature was very cruel. Then I began to realize that my love was undergoing discipline; that I was to expand my love, not limit it to my family. God showed me that it was He whom I loved in my loved ones. Then, from within, my love began to expand to all. I could no longer feel partiality toward family. When I returned to India in 1935, I saw that this was true....

Therefore, through family life and then through national life, God is schooling every individual to understand his international family, that we may have a United States of the World with Truth as our guide.

International Understanding Dissolves Divisive Boundaries

We are all aliens here. No territory belongs permanently to any country. The hand of time eventually erases all nations. Their boundaries don't last, because they represent divisions that have been carved out by force. I believe a time will come when in greater understanding we shall have no boundaries anymore. We shall call the earth our country; and we shall, by a process of justice and international assembly, distribute unselfishly the goods of the world according to the needs of the people. But equality cannot be established by force; it must come from the heart. The greatest blessing would be to develop international understanding by which we may realize this truth.

These ideals should be taught in all the schools. Just as it would be a sin to teach everyone to "love your family; it doesn't matter what happens to your country," so it is a sin to teach love of country that militates against your greater world family. When in every school love of country is overemphasized, it sows the seeds of misunderstanding and even hatred toward other nations. How dare we spoil children by teaching them the kind of patriotism in which there are seeds of hatred! Unless you love your country, you cannot love the world; but children should be taught also to love other countries as they love their own. That is the principle of God.

PEACE WILL COME WHEN WE LEARN TO SEE GOD IN ALL

So you see, we must dissociate our wisdom from all environmental influences. If we can learn to understand others, and to free our minds from all prejudices born of environment, we begin to express the perfect image of God within us and to find it in all. "But as many as received him, to them gave he power to become the sons of God."* The light of the sun falls equally on the diamond and the charcoal; but the diamond, by its transparency, reflects the sun more. Bhagavan Krishna taught that because the wisdom in man is covered by ignorance, and because man chooses to misuse his independence to nurture that ignorance, he doesn't reflect the true image of God that is within him. But in all those who use the power of the mind to be good, the power of Spirit will manifest.† If we can *receive* that power of Spirit, then we become true sons of God. And we must learn to see the light of God falling on both His good and bad children. Peace will come when we discipline our hearts to see God in all, not just in those who love us or whom we think of as our own.

Peace is not something that you and I or a few great souls can create at once, by command. Even a million Christs or Krishnas could not do it. Try as he would, Lord Krishna could not prevent the great war between the Pandavas and Kauravas, which is described in the *Mahabharata*.‡ All humanity has to become Christlike to bring peace on earth. When each one of us shapes his life according to

---

* John 1:12.

† "Wisdom is eclipsed by cosmic delusion; mankind is thereby bewildered. But in those who have banished ignorance by Self-knowledge, their wisdom, like the illuminating sun, makes manifest the Supreme Self" (*God Talks With Arjuna:The Bhagavad Gita* V:15-16).

‡ Hindu epic poem, of which the Bhagavad Gita is a part.

the wisdom and example of a Christ, a Krishna, a Buddha, we can have peace here; not before. We must start now, with ourselves. We should try to be like the divine ones who have come on earth again and again to show us the way. By our loving each other and keeping our understanding clear, as they taught and exemplified, peace can come.

Peace Begins at Home and in the Schools

Each individual in a family and community should strive to live peacefully with others. Peace must begin in the home and in the schools. In the classrooms we must teach international patriotism — to love the world as Jesus, Krishna, and the great masters have taught, and not to do anything that would lead to international discomfort. It is not our nationality or our color that we should be proud of, but our understanding. We should cultivate our understanding and use it to determine what is truly best for family happiness, national happiness, and international happiness. International happiness should include the well-being of the nation, the community, and the family. The standard of legislation should be merit, not color of skin or any other class distinction. These are the ideals to be taught to children.

So long as God's children differentiate, "We are Indians and you are Americans; we are Germans, you are English," so long will they be bound by delusion and the world divided. Much war and suffering and destruction will be prevented if we cease to emphasize differences and learn to love all without distinction or prejudice. Be more proud that you are made in the image of God than that you are of a certain nationality; for "American" and "Indian" and all the other nationalities are just outer coats, which in time will be discarded. But you are a child of God throughout eternity. Isn't it better to teach that ideal to your children? It is the only way to peace: Establish the true ideals of peace in the schools, and live peace in your own life....

YOGA MEDITATION REVEALS
OUR DIVINE NATURE

Out of the cosmic tomes of truth, India developed the Yoga system, the science of oneness — oneness of the soul with God; oneness with the principles of eternal righteousness; with the universe; and with all mankind. The sage Patanjali formulated the Yoga system into eight steps for achieving the goal:

1. Avoid unrighteous behavior — *yama*.
2. Follow certain moral and spiritual precepts — *niyama*.
3. Learn to be still in body and mind, for where motion ceases, there begins the perception of God — *asana*.
4. While concentrating on the state of peace,

practice control of the life force in the body —*pranayama*.

5. When your mind is your own, that is, under your control through *pranayama,* then you can give it to God —*pratyahara*.

6. Then begins meditation: first, concentrate on one of God's cosmic manifestations such as love, wisdom, joy —*dharana*.

7. What follows in meditation is an expansion of the realization of God's infinite om- nipresent nature —*dhyana*.

8. When the soul merges as one with God, who is ever-existing, ever-conscious, ever- new Bliss, that is the goal —*samadhi*.

The joy of God can never be exhausted. He is sufficient; the purpose and the aim of existence. True understanding comes when we feel God as the great bliss of meditation. And peace is the first proof of His presence.

To have peace we must love more, but we can- not love people unconditionally unless we know God. The soul is absolutely perfect, but when identified with the body as ego, its expression be- comes distorted by human imperfections. If hu- man beings were only these imperfect bodies and minds, there would be some justification for prej- udices and divisions. But we are all souls, made in God's image. So Yoga teaches us to know the di- vine nature in ourselves and others. Through yoga meditation we can know that we are gods.

IF EVERYONE LEARNS GOD-COMMUNION, PEACE WILL REIGN

I believe that if every citizen in the world is taught to *commune* with God (not merely to know Him intellectually), then peace can reign; not before. When by persistence in meditation you realize God through communion with Him, your heart is prepared to embrace all humanity.

I am neither a Hindu nor an American. Humanity is my race, and no one on earth can make me feel otherwise. Prejudice and exclusiveness are so childish. We are here for just a little while and then whisked away. We must remember only that we are children of God. I love all countries as I love my India. And my prayer to you is that you love all nations as you love America. God created a diverse world to teach you to forget your physical differences with other races; and, from the debris of misunderstanding and prejudice, to salvage your understanding and use it to make an effort to know Him as our one Father.

Therefore, my friends, resolve that you will love the world as your own nation, and that you will love your nation as you love your family. Through this understanding you will help to establish a world family on the indestructible foundation of wisdom.

Follow the ways of God. Set a time apart each day to meditate on Him. When you commune with God, you shall feel toward everyone as toward your own. No one can ever make me feel he is not mine. All human beings are God's children, and He is my Father.

Is Peace Possible
in Today's World?

By Brother Anandamoy

Considering the turmoil and suffering caused by the conflicts throughout the world today, it is natural to think how nice it would be if God would simply intervene and put a stop to war. However, when we look at the real causes of war, we see that it is a very complex problem — one that can be solved only through deep understanding and individual spiritual growth.

In the following words, Paramahansa Yogananda touches on three basic points that are vital for understanding the causes of war:

> Since God has given all men the power to do their own thinking and initiate their own actions, He and the great saints who commune with Him do not in any way interfere with man's individual freedom. Both men and nations must reap good or bad results of their actions, initiated by their use or misuse of free choice.

Condensed from a talk given at Self-Realization Fellowship Temple, Pasadena, California. The entire talk is available on audiocassette.

God and the holy men who are filled with divine power do not come out of the clouds and use magnetic force to electrocute wrongdoers in times of war. To do so would be a contradiction, nullifying the free choice with which the Heavenly Father has endowed His children. The divinely bestowed power of human beings to act freely would be rendered meaningless. God does not use His almighty power to forcibly stop world evils, nor should we expect great masters who know Him, and who are in tune with His wishes, to use their miraculous powers to stop them, for to do so would go against the divine plan for the evolution of man through free choice.

Let us look at each of these three key points: First, human beings have free will and reason, with which no lower form of life is endowed. God does not interfere with that freedom. The second point is the role of karma, the law of cause and effect, which makes us reap the results of our use of free will. But even that doesn't give the whole picture. The third and most important point in this subject — the most subtle and least understood — is "the divine plan for the evolution of man through free choice." I want to explain each of these principles, because they make the problem of war much more understandable.

SEEING BEYOND SUPERFICIAL CAUSES

In trying to comprehend world events, most people think only in terms of what is immediately obvious. They see, for example, the leaders of one nation doing something hostile or threatening to another nation, and believe that this causes war. But there is always a deeper reason than the isolated incidents and temporary pattern of current events. Let me give you an example.

In the eighteenth century, there was a war between two tiny states in Europe — Corsica and the city-state of Genoa. Do you know what started that war? The history books say it was a peasant who had failed to pay all his taxes. Because he was short a half-penny, he was imprisoned; and this so inflamed nationalistic passions that war was declared. It lasted forty-four years and cost eighty thousand lives. Now, do you think the origin of a war that lasted so long and cost so many lives was one half-penny? Impossible! The true cause was the accumulated bad karma of those particular groups of people. By wrong thoughts and actions, those nations had put themselves out of harmony with the universal order, and war was the natural result according to the divine law of cause and effect.

Transgression of Divine Laws

Newspapers and history books deal with the events that are the superficial causes of war. But the real explanation is to be found in the abuse of spiritual principles. There was a saint in Italy, Padre Pio, whom I have had the opportunity of visiting. Shortly before his death in 1968, an American journalist went to see him, and asked, "What is the cause of all the turmoil and trouble in the world today?" And Padre Pio replied, "Moral degeneration!" Then the newspaperman asked him, "And what is the cure?" Padre Pio answered, "Holy fear of God." The Self-Realization teachings say the same thing, but in different terms: "Go back to living in harmony with the laws of God; love God and seek Him in meditation. That is the cure for all ills in this world, including war."

Look at the Civil War in America, for example. Historians ascribe that war to the dispute over slavery, and to deep political and economic tensions between the industrial North and the agricultural South. But Abraham Lincoln, who was a very spiritual man with profound understanding, discerned the true cause. This is what he said:

> Insomuch as we know that by divine law nations, like individuals, are subjected to punishments and chastisements in this world, may we not justly fear that the awful calamity of civil war which now desolates the land may be but a punishment inflicted upon us for our presumptuous sins, to the need of our national reformation as a whole people?
>
> We have been the recipients of the choicest bounties of heaven. We have been preserved these many years in peace and prosperity. We have grown in numbers, in wealth and power as no other nation has grown. But we have forgotten God. We have forgotten the gracious Hand which preserved us in peace and multiplied and

enriched and strengthened us. And we have imagined, in the deceitfulness of our hearts, that all these blessings were produced by some superior wisdom and virtue of our own. Intoxicated with unbroken success, we have become too self-sufficient to feel the need of redeeming and preserving grace, too proud to pray to the God that made us.*

THE DIVINE PLAN FOR OUR EVOLUTION

War comes not only as karmic punishment; more important, as Paramahansa Yogananda pointed out in the passage quoted earlier, is "the divine plan for the evolution of man." Lincoln was referring to this when he talked about "the need of our national reformation as a whole people."

Do you see how the divine plan works for our continuous evolution toward oneness with God? If we misuse our judgment and free will, and are foolish enough to go against God's laws, those laws still operate for our highest good, bringing us experiences that prod us (through suffering if necessary) into making the effort to recover our lost harmony with the Divine. Eventually, we come to understand: "*I* am the cause of my own suffering. *I* have to change. I *can* change and gradually transcend all these limitations and evils."

---

* From Lincoln's proclamation of a national day of fasting and prayer, April 30, 1863.

WORLD PEACE COMES ONLY THROUGH
INDIVIDUAL PEACE

In one sense, we can compare the world situation to the human body. When the cells are healthy, the organs are healthy; and when the organs are well, the whole body is filled with vitality. But if something is wrong with the cells, then the health of the entire body goes.

So it is with civilization as a whole. As long as individuals live in harmony with themselves and their families, the automatic result is peace and harmony on the national and global level. And if the individual is full of greed, selfishness, and hatred, this manifests as war and struggle on the social level. Whether a person fights with his bare hands, with speech, or just in thought, or whether nations fight with guided missiles, the underlying cause is the same: selfishness, egotism. Therefore, to bring peace in the world, we have to change as individuals. We have to live according to the laws of God.

THE UNIVERSAL WAR BETWEEN
GOOD AND EVIL

This solution may sound simple, even simplistic; yet it is one of the most difficult things for us to achieve. Why is this so? Why is it seemingly so natural for human beings to feel anger, hatred, and the other evil impulses that produce inharmony and war?

As long as our consciousness is identified with this world, we will be subject to negative influences, because evil is inherent in the very fabric of creation.* Considering this, we can see that the answer to our question, "Why doesn't God stop war?" is ultimately very simple: God does not stop war because He started it — at the very beginning of creation, in the opposing forces of duality. Out of His undifferentiated consciousness He projected the force of *maya,* or cosmic delusion, that manifested this whole universe and gave it the illusory appearance of being separate from Him. However, there is also a counterforce in this dualistic universe; the outgoing energy of *maya* is at war with the unifying power of divine love that draws all finite things back to their source in the Infinite Consciousness.

This cosmic war is the "plot" of God's dream-picture of creation. So we can see why a saint in India said:

> "World" means ceaseless movement, and obviously there can be no rest in movement. How could there be peace in perpetual coming and going? Peace reigns where there is no motion, no duality. Reverse your course. Advance toward God. And then there will be hope for peace....As long as one's real home has not been found, suffering is inevitable. The sense of

---

* "Evil had to be, if there was to be any creation. If you wrote a message with white chalk on a white board, no one would see it....Without shadows as well as light there could be no picture. Evil is the shadow that converts the one beam of God's light into pictures or forms."—Paramahansa Yogananda, *The Divine Romance*

separateness [from God] is the root cause of all misery.

This is a very deep point: Real peace can be found only when our consciousness transcends the dualities of this world — light and darkness, pleasure and pain, health and sickness, life and death, war and peace — by regaining the unity of God-consciousness. And just as on the universal level there is constant war between the outgoing force of *maya,* which keeps us caught up in the outer dualistic show, and the ingoing force of divine love, which is seeking to draw us back to union with God, so in our individual consciousness that same battle is being fought.

Yoga—Inner Victory Over the Cause of War

Goethe had his character Faust say, "Two souls I have within my bosom." What he expressed poetically, yoga explains scientifically: Opposing the divine consciousness of the soul within each of us is the ego, the lower self or pseudo-soul. We can see this battle between spiritual qualities and materialistic habits in ourselves countless times each day. For example, when you feel, "I should meditate," the ego counters by urging, "No, let's watch TV." The divine Self says, "Eat moderately and eat only healthful food." The ego says, "No, I want chocolate cake and ice cream, and the more the better." When the ego is winning, the individual is dominated by selfishness, anger, greed — all the things that bind us to the delusion of mortal consciousness.

When the majority of society is in the grip of these negative forces, war is inevitable; I think this is quite easy to understand. But there is a deeper aspect to the inner battle between ego consciousness and divine consciousness, which most people do not comprehend. That aspect holds the practical key to solving the problem of war and suffering; it can be grasped only through the science of yoga. Paramahansa Yogananda has explained:

> There are two currents flowing in the body.* One is from the point between the eyebrows to the coccyx. This downwardly flowing or *apana* current has for its center the coccyx, through which it distributes itself to the sensory nerves and keeps the consciousness of man delusively tied to the body. The *apana* current, therefore, is restless and engrosses man in sensory experiences. There is another current, called *prana,* which is flowing from the coccyx to the point between the eyebrows. The nature of this life-current is calm; it withdraws inwardly the attention of the soul...and unites the soul with Spirit....There is an opposite pull exercised by the downwardly flowing current as compared to the upwardly flowing current. The soul's attention is often being pulled upward or downward by these two currents. In other words,

---

* Paramahansaji explained elsewhere that the life-energy, or *prana,* in the body becomes specialized in five principal currents. In this context, he refers to specific functions related to the two currents called *prana* and *apana.*

there is a tug-of-war between these two forces
to take the soul downward or upward. Owing to
the opposite pull of these two currents, the ex-
halation and inhalations of breath are born.

Do you understand what this means? With
every breath we take, there is a subtle war going
on within us, between spiritual consciousness and
material consciousness. As long as those currents
are pulling against each other, which happens as
long as we are breathing, we are in body consciousness, ego consciousness. In his *Autobiography of a Yogi* the Master explains this subtle principle further:

> The breath and the restless mind, I saw, are like
> two storms that lash the ocean of light into
> waves of material forms — earth, sky, human be-
> ings, animals, birds, trees. No perception of the
> Infinite as One Light can be had except by calm-
> ing those two storms [through practice of sci-
> entific meditation]. As often as I quieted the two
> natural tumults, I beheld the multitudinous
> waves of creation melt into one lucent sea; even
> as the waves of the ocean, when a tempest sub-
> sides, serenely dissolve into unity.

Though these ideas may seem very deep, they
are essential for understanding the root cause of
war and the way to peace. Remember, war is the
karmic result of man's misuse of free will, his transgression of divine law. That misuse of free choice
comes about because of the evil influence of *maya,*
the cosmic force of delusion that makes human beings forget their divine nature and become egotisti-

cally identified with the outer world. Entrapment in delusion can be overcome only by reversing the outward flow of consciousness and energy in the body through scientific spiritual techniques, so that we become aware of our inner oneness with God. It is only in that state of divine consciousness that selfishness, anger, hatred and all the other causes of war are permanently overcome.

Understanding the Purpose of Life

Let me develop further the third vital principle I mentioned earlier, "the divine plan for the evolution of man through free will." The divine plan for humanity is, first of all, that we learn to use our God-given free will and reason in a constructive way, in harmony with God's laws. But that is not the end. The next step, which every one of us must take sooner or later, is to learn through meditation to calm the inner storms of restlessness. When we make peace in that war which is going on within us all the time, we realize what we really are. We are not this body, this world of duality is not our home; we are the soul, and our home is in God's consciousness. It is delusion, it is the ego, that tells us we are this flesh and this personality, subject to limitations, suffering, and evil.

So we should not remain wholly engrossed in externals, and in worrying about the world situation: "What is going to happen?" or "If only this person or that leader would act differently, the world would be so much better." Certainly, we should keep abreast of current events, and do our part to improve world conditions. But we have to realize that the way we can contribute most effectively to world peace is to live in peace within ourselves, and that comes only by overcoming the ego — its selfishness, greed, and so on.

I want to quote a doctor who was president of a college in Minnesota:*

> I do not believe the greatest threat to our future is from bombs or guided missiles. I don't think our civilization will die that way. It will die when we no longer care, when the spiritual forces that make us wish to be right and noble die in the hearts of men. Arnold Toynbee has pointed out that nineteen of twenty-one notable civilizations have died from within, and not by conquest from without. There were no bands playing and no flags waving when these civilizations decayed. It happened slowly, in the quiet and the dark, when no one was aware. If America is to grow great, we must stop gagging at the word 'spiritual.' Our task is to rediscover and reassert our faith in the spiritual, the spiritual values on which American life has really rested from its beginning.

Our culture today emphasizes the importance of satisfying the ego through material pleasures. According to an article I read recently, Americans spend eighty billion dollars a year on illegal drugs! There is an endless search for amusements, and popular entertainment today is generally not very

* Dr. Laurence Gould, Carleton College.

inspiring; it rarely brings out the positive, spiritual, noble side of our nature. More often it is violence for violence's sake; sensationalism; things that rouse the lower emotions. This leads to moral degeneration — and to destruction. If people only understood that, they wouldn't be so surprised by the turmoil and unrest in the world today.

So many people say, "Yes, we want peace." But if you ask them why, too often the answer is, "So that we can live a comfortable life and 'do our own thing'"— pleasing the senses and ego through a materialistic life. We must learn to ask, "What is the purpose of life? Why are we here?" Are we here to work for peace merely so that we can indulge the ego? No. The purpose of life is to realize what we really are: the immortal soul, one with God. We are not meant to have a perfect earth, but to learn that our home lies beyond the dualities of this world — pleasure and pain, riches and poverty, war and peace, life and death. That liberating realization is the divine plan for each of us, and it is the only workable answer to the threat of war. Think about it.

Some years ago, when I was minister at the Self-Realization Fellowship Lake Shrine, we had three pairs of swans: The first pair was white, another was black, and the third was white with black necks. They all fought with each other — not just skirmishing, but fighting to *kill*. Finally we had to build screens to divide the lake into three sections to separate the swans. The lake was plenty big enough for all of them, but each pair wanted it wholly for themselves. And I thought, "They are just like people!" As long as selfishness is present, as long as even one party wants "the whole cake," there is going to be war.

If everyone would live according to the laws of God and try to overcome selfishness, considering the welfare of others, we would eventually have world peace. But people on this earth are not all on the same level of understanding. This has nothing to do with nationality or race, as some people say; it is a matter of individual spiritual evolution. It is just like school: Some people are in kindergarten, some are in grade school, some are in high school, and some are at the university level. We simply cannot expect that everybody will have enough spiritual understanding to see the necessity for unselfishly regarding the welfare of others.

Because of this, there is much controversy nowadays over the correct approach to peace. Some say, "We should build up our armed forces in order to become stronger; this will act as a deterrent to war." Others want to disarm; they say, "Let's follow Gandhi's example and practice nonviolence." Who is right?

INSIGHT FROM THE BIBLE AND BHAGAVAD GITA

Let us discuss what the scriptures have to say on the subject of war. In the Bible and in the Bhagavad Gita, the great scriptures on which the Self-Realization teachings are founded, we find two different aspects of this question addressed.

In a well-known passage from the gospel of St. Matthew, Jesus says: "All they that take the sword shall perish with the sword." Commenting on these words, Paramahansa Yogananda wrote:

> Jesus prophesied to individuals and nations of the world that those who believe in the power of swords will ultimately perish by the sword. Modern gangsters who keep themselves constantly armed with guns, and who are ready to use them, almost invariably find themselves sooner or later killed by gunshots. Modern-style warfare conclusively proves that aggressive wars of conquest bring to the invaders losses as grievous as those of the invaded.

This is very interesting, because Paramahansaji wrote this before atom bombs came into being. He went on to say:

> According to human nature, anyone who in anger or through some other evil influence, lashes his sword against his enemy will find a sword drawn against himself. Hatred rouses hatred. A man of murderous inclination attracts the same evil vibration like a boomerang against himself. All conquerors and aggressive nations, take heed, for those who use the sword shall perish by the sword. The sword often defeats the purpose for which it was used, whereas love, when used wisely, never fails to produce the desired result.

Sometimes people feel there is a contradiction in the teachings of Christ. For instance, Jesus advocated nonviolence when he taught, "Turn the other cheek." He was pointing out that if we retaliate with anger and hatred, expressing our ego, we are out of harmony with spiritual law and thus cause trouble for ourselves. Jesus himself practiced nonviolence in the highest way when he allowed himself to be crucified. But when he saw that certain leaders were influencing the population in evil ways, he was not quiet. When principles of righteousness were at stake, he fought — vigorously!*

There is a parallel in the life of the Lord Krishna, the Christ of India. His friends, the Pandava brothers, had by deceit been sent into exile for thirteen years; and during their absence a very unrighteous man, Duryodhana, ruled their kingdom. It was understood that after the exile, Yudhisthira, the eldest Pandava brother, would regain his rulership of the country. But when they returned, Duryodhana would not relinquish the throne. War was brewing between the two factions, and Krishna tried his utmost to negotiate a peaceful settlement. But when Duryodhana refused to cooperate, war was the only alternative.

---

* "And when he had made a scourge of small cords, he drove them [the moneychangers] all out of the temple, and the sheep, and the oxen, and poured out the changers' money, and overthrew the tables" (John 2:14). "Think not that I am come to send peace on earth: I came not to send peace, but a sword" (Matthew 10:34).

WHEN IS IT OUR DUTY TO FIGHT?

It was on the eve of that great war, on the battle-field of Kurukshetra, that Krishna gave the discourse recorded in the Bhagavad Gita. Standing between the two armies, the Pandava prince Arjuna had said to Krishna, "I do not want to fight; I'm sick of all the killing. Let Duryodhana have the kingdom. I don't want it, and my brother doesn't want it, if it means so much bloodshed and destruction in the land."

But then Krishna explained to him: "It is your duty to fight. The issue is not a personal matter of whether or not your older brother wants to be king. It is a question of the welfare of the whole country. As long as this unrighteous man is ruling, the entire population will suffer. On the other hand, if the country is ruled by your brother, who is the embodiment of righteousness, all will bene-fit. Therefore, it is your duty as a *kshatriya* to fight. This is a righteous war."

"Kshatriya" refers to one of the four Hindu castes — that of rulers and warriors, whose duty it is to defend the country and keep peace. It is im-portant to realize that the caste system, as it has been practiced in recent centuries, is a gross dis-tortion of the true significance of the castes. The real caste system, as it was understood in the higher ages, was not based on inheritance or social status, but was a means of classifying individuals according to their temperament, natural abilities, and state of spiritual evolution. And it is very interesting to note

that although the caste system was introduced thousands of years ago in an age of enlightenment, there was always a warrior caste. Even in the highest ages, there was usually some rascal around who created trouble and war. Often those people were very powerful individuals — so much so that from time to time a divine incarnation had to come to restore peace and harmony in the world.

Lord Krishna says in the Bhagavad Gita: "O Arjuna, fortunate are the *kshatriyas* who are summoned to fight in a righteous battle that they have not provoked. A righteous battle verily opens the door to heaven." Commenting on Krishna's words, Paramahansa Yogananda said: "According to the law of karma, a man who dies courageously on the battlefield with a clear conscience" — meaning that he did not instigate the war, that he is not the aggressor, and has no hatred in his heart; he is simply defending his country — "attains a blissful state after death and is reborn on earth with a valiant mind in a noble family."

THE TRUE MEANING OF NONVIOLENCE

Now, you may ask, "Isn't that contrary to the principles of nonviolence taught by Christ, and in our time, by Gandhi?" No, it is not. Krishna also taught nonviolence, giving utmost importance to overcoming anger, hatred, greed, selfishness — those qualities of the ego or lower self that are the causes of war. Krishna was bringing out a vital point about nonviolence: There are times when it is our spiritual duty to fight. This was also understood by Jesus and Mahatma Gandhi, as Paramahansa Yogananda explained:

> Gandhi maintains that it is better to resist with physical force than to be a coward. If a man and his family, for example, are attacked by a criminal who levels his gun at them, and the man, being actuated by inward fear, says, "Gunman, I forgive you for whatever you may do," and then flies away, these actions cannot be called a display of nonviolence, but of cowardice. According to Gandhi, a man in such a situation should resort even to force, rather than hide his act of cowardice under a mask of nonviolence. To return a slap for a slap is easy, but more difficult it is to resist a slap by love. Any warrior who uses physical or spiritual force to defend a righteous cause always derives in his soul a heavenly satisfaction.

I think many people have a rather naive understanding of what nonviolence entails. Nonviolence —*ahimsa* in Sanskrit — means more than just not killing; it means not to harm anyone in action, in speech, or in thought. Those of us who are practicing Raja Yoga should think deeply about this, because *ahimsa* is part of the very first step of Raja Yoga.*

---

* The Raja Yoga system of Patanjali is known as the Eightfold Path (see pages 159–160). The first steps are (1) *yama* (moral conduct), and (2) *niyama* (religious observances). *Yama* is fulfilled by noninjury to others, truthfulness, nonstealing, continence, and noncovetousness. The *niyama* prescripts are purity of body and mind, contentment in all circumstances, self-discipline, self-study (contemplation), and devotion to God and guru.

The other rules of *yama* and *niyama* that are part of that first step — honesty, overcoming greed and selfishness, living a disciplined, moral life, and so on — are the guidelines whose practice enable us to understand what nonviolence means. As long as one is dishonest, greedy, selfish in his personal life, or violates moral laws, he is violent — even if outwardly he says, "I am not going to fight."

SELF-DISCIPLINE IS ESSENTIAL
TO NONVIOLENCE

One saint in India said, "As long as a person does not have inner harmony, as long as he is in inner turmoil, he is hurting others that are in his environment, even though he is engaged in service outwardly." Do you see how subtle and far-reaching it is?

Nonviolence is not merely saying: "I do not want to go to war; I do not want to fight." A person's aversion to fighting may be based on a totally selfish motivation: "I do not want to undergo the hardships of war; I do not want to risk my life." This is not *ahimsa. Ahimsa* is a spiritual force that is built only through tremendous spiritual, moral, intellectual, and emotional self-discipline.* In the truly nonvio-

---

* In an article in the Spring 1983 issue of *Self-Realization,* Professor Michael N. Nagler, an expert on Gandhi at the University of California at Berkeley, wrote: "It is sometimes overlooked, behind the glamour of Gandhi's personality and the drama of the Indian situation, that fifteen or twenty years of dogged, almost military self-discipline lay behind the conversion of ordinary Indian women and men into an irresistible flood of love that broke down the barriers of imperialism."

lent person, the power of love has become stronger than the instinct of self-preservation. That is no simple transformation, for self-preservation is normally the strongest impulse in human nature.

In *Autobiography of a Yogi,* the Master talks about *satyagraha* ("holding to truth"), which is the movement Gandhi introduced. He mentions the vows taken by the *satyagrahis* (the earnest followers of Gandhi). Those vows included nonviolence, truthfulness, nonstealing, celibacy, nonpossession, physical labor, control of the palate, fearlessness, equal respect for all religions, freedom from untouchability. All these vows were to be observed in a spirit of humility. So this principle of nonviolence, of *ahimsa,* is a very deep one, and is based on tremendous discipline.

Albert Schweitzer was another who exemplified the spirit of *ahimsa.* He called it "reverence for all life," and lived by the truth that life is one. It is the one God who has taken on the forms of all. So if we are fighting, it means we are doing violence against our own Self. Essentially, we are one.

IS WESTERN SOCIETY READY TO PRACTICE NONVIOLENCE?

With this in mind, let us look at the West. Are we ready to practice nonviolence? First, consider television. Look at the incredible violence depicted in popular shows. This influence subtly (and sometimes not so subtly) conditions the viewer's consciousness — not only adults, but particularly children. In a recent report on the psychological and social influence of television, the Surgeon General of the United States said: "Television enters powerfully into the learning process of children, and teaches them a set of moral and social values about violence which are inconsistent with the standards of a civilized society." We cannot expect children to see violence on television and not be influenced. Their receptive minds absorb those vibrations. How could a nation practice nonviolence when its children, its future citizens and leaders, are raised and nurtured on violence?

Secondly, if we look at politics, business, and society in general, we see that everybody is fighting like those swans I told you about. It seems that people are becoming increasingly inconsiderate of the welfare of others. The racial discrimination that is still going on to a great extent; the cheating in business, in politics, in personal relationships, are all violations of the principle of nonviolence. Think of the large number of weapons in the hands of private citizens. People may not use them, but the mere fact that they have them is latent violence. The breaking of moral laws, the incredible number of babies born out of wedlock, and so on — these actions are in conflict with the fundamental moral structure of the universe, and inevitably set up vibrations of inharmony in ourselves and our environment.* We cannot go against the laws of God and say, "I am nonviolent."

The appalling number of divorces today is also caused by violations of this spiritual principle of nonviolence. One expert on marriage stated: "Marriage is always work, especially when the partners are strong-willed and exacting." Speaking of the conflicts in his own marriage, he said: "In each case of [my] fighting with my wife, she was angry at me for neglecting her. She was saying, 'You don't care about me. You only think of yourself.'" And then he said, based not only on his personal experience, but that of countless people who have come to him for counseling: "Married couples are continually crying to each other for attention, for reassurance"—meaning, for friendship and support. "Marriages endure when these cries are answered, and break up when they are not. The anger behind most quarrels, of course, comes from the feeling that the marriage has lost its savor and excitement."

What does this mean? Simply that those marriages are not based on the proper foundation of friendship, of mutual help, of mutual support, of unselfishness. The result is abuse—physical, mental, and emotional. In one word: violence.

If we analyze it in this way, it is clear that we are living in a violent society. When we talk about peace in the world, usually we are thinking in terms of what the governments and leaders of na-

---

* "The cosmic order *(rita)* that upholds the universe is not different from the moral order that rules man's destiny."—Paramahansa Yogananda

tions should do. This is unrealistic. We, as individuals, are the ones who have work to do. As long as there is no peace in our community, in our family, in ourselves, we cannot expect to have peace in the world. Outer conditions in the world are simply a reflection of the inner state of individuals.

FREEDOM IS THE BIRTHRIGHT OF THE SOUL

Let me read to you a news report from 1950:

In a spirit of international friendship, a group of over three hundred friends of India met in Los Angeles on January 26, to celebrate India's birth as a republic....A rapt audience heard Paramahansa Yogananda's plea for world brotherhood. Speaking of India's new status he said:

"The Indian republic has been a dream I have cherished from infancy. Those who have not suffered political fetters cannot imagine my feelings tonight. India loves her freedom, England loves her freedom, America loves her freedom, all nations love their freedom; it is the birthright of the soul. But in the pursuit of this freedom, we become divided. Atom bombs will not bring it; atom bombs will bring only more destruction, more suspicion and fear. The physical forces are teaching us that unless we employ them for constructive purposes, we shall never have happiness and freedom. This is not a time for hate and division. We have our choice: to live in fear of an atom bomb, or to live in love and brotherhood....We must have one world, one race of God, one religion of love. God is our Father, and we are His children. He has created the dark and the yellow and the white. Let no man be proud of his skin, but of God's one light shining in the multicolored lamps of flesh."

This is an appeal to the whole world. It is an appeal for brotherhood and peace. But we should remember what the Master says here: "Those who have not suffered political fetters cannot imagine what I feel." Many people take their freedom for granted, particularly in America. Those of you who have not known what it means to live under political oppression cannot conceive what it is like. You cannot fully appreciate what freedom means.

I grew up in Switzerland, and there the ideal of freedom was pounded into us from babyhood. Before and during World War II, I saw how people were persecuted under the Nazi regime, people who fled into Switzerland, leaving everything behind. A good friend of mine, whose whole family had died in a concentration camp, told me, "You have no idea what it meant to me and others to come into a land where we can be free!" And consider the Pilgrims who came to America, to a new country where there was nothing but wilderness, where they had to start their lives all over. They did not mind it because they had freedom.

I am not speaking politically; I am speaking of spiritual principles — the same principles upheld by Jesus when he fought against unrighteousness and by Krishna when he encouraged Arjuna to go to war. Of course, politically both sides think their cause is a righteous one, so the question always arises, "Who is right?" The Master says, "God knows who is right and who is wrong. Let us all be united in everything that is noble." He had a great love for America, and once said:

> Uphold the ideals of this country.* If ever aggressive war came to destroy this country and America needed my help, I would give it for the love of the people and to defend the nation on whose land I live. We should do our part to help protect America and all those we love, but at the same time we must not allow ourselves to be filled with hatred. Never has the world needed love as much as now. Love will be the potent factor in eradicating war.

And he doesn't stop there. He goes on to say, "Let us all resolve that no matter what happens, we make God the polestar of our lives, and that we will send that love to all."

PEACE WILL COME AS INDIVIDUALS CHANGE

Here we have the essential point: Each of us has a responsibility to live in harmony with God. People who think peace and security are simply a

---

* On another occasion, Paramahansaji wrote: "I love and support that hundred percent Americanism which excludes all superstition, meaningless dogma, untruth, and unkindness to brother nations; which is solely and wholly founded on lasting principles of truth, true patriotism, and international, interracial, and interreligious tolerance and goodwill to all."

matter of building up military forces are wholly missing the fundamental principle. Armament for defensive purposes certainly has its place. But the deciding factor in the issue of international peace is whether or not we are living according to the laws of God, because war and natural calamities are always caused by man's transgression of God's laws.

We cannot simply leave it up to the politicians. Some people are waiting for better leaders to be voted into office, thinking that world conditions would then improve. We must realize that it is the karma of each nation — the sum total of good and evil thoughts and actions of the population — that selects its leaders. So if we are not satisfied with the leaders of our country, it means we have work to do on ourselves.

In *Autobiography of a Yogi* the Master says:

> The Biblical story of Abraham's plea to the Lord* that the city of Sodom be spared if ten righteous men could be found therein, and the Divine Reply: "I will not destroy it for ten's sake," gains new meaning in the light of India's escape from oblivion. Gone are the empires of mighty nations, skilled in the arts of war, that once were India's contemporaries: ancient Egypt, Babylonia, Greece, Rome.
>
> The Lord's answer clearly shows that a land lives, not in its material achievements, but in its masterpieces of man.

* Genesis 18:23-32.

Let the divine words be heard again, in this twentieth century, twice dyed in blood ere half over: No nation that can produce ten men who are great in the eyes of the Unbribable Judge shall know extinction.

Heeding such persuasions, India has proved herself not witless against the thousand cunnings of Time. Self-realized masters in every century have hallowed her soil. Modern Christlike sages, like Lahiri Mahasaya and Sri Yukteswar, rise up to proclaim that a knowledge of yoga, the science of God-realization, is vital to man's happiness and to a nation's longevity.

In another place the Master says, "Hundreds of thousands, not dozens merely, of Kriya Yogis are needed to bring into manifestation the world of peace and plenty that awaits men when they have made the proper effort to reestablish their status as sons of the divine Father." Of course, it's not just Kriya Yogis; other good people are following true spiritual paths, living the spiritual life. The point made by Paramahansaji is that we have to go back to the laws of God, and to our true relationship with Him. Our Guru emphasizes Kriya Yoga because this science is the most direct approach to reestablishing our attunement with God and realizing our true soul nature. To the degree that we experience the love and joy which are innate to the soul, our egoistic desires and selfishness automatically and correspondingly disappear; we then have a new set of values.

People seek more and more material possessions

because their soul inherently possesses everything. Through external means the soul is unconsciously trying to express its omniscience, omnipotence, and omnipresence. But as long as people believe that they can satisfy the soul's craving through material things, there will naturally be conflicts with others over riches and power. Thus wars will continue. Peace will come when we learn that fulfillment lies not in possessions. It will come when we realize that the external world is simply God's drama in which we are meant to learn that regardless of what temporary role we are playing, we are eternally the children of God, heirs to His kingdom of all-fulfillment. Only through the inner attainment of divine consciousness can we find that fulfillment.

As more people will come to that realization, and as a consequence live according to the divine laws of righteousness, gradually peace will come. When we make the effort to change ourselves spiritually, we are helping not only ourselves, but also our families and all with whom we come in contact, as well as our country and the whole world.

So there is the answer. Is peace possible today? It is possible, if everyone cooperates by changing themselves so that they express in a greater way the innate qualities of their true divine nature.

Change Yourself, Transform the World

By Sri Mrinalini Mata

Many noble ideas have been propounded in this world by great men and women. There have been numerous worthwhile institutions and societies founded on the strong and pure foundation of the beautiful ideals and inspiration of the individuals who gave them birth. But succeeding generations of leaders and followers sometimes dilute and diffuse the original intent and message. For a society to persist in its pristine purity, its followers must truly emulate its founder.

It is not enough that the mind be stimulated by the scriptures, inspired momentarily to do a little bit of good in this world, or to lead a moral existence. What is necessary is that souls be so deeply inspired by truth and by the example of the great saints who have known how to commune with God, how to realize He is a part of their very own

Extracts from a talk given at Yogoda Satsanga Society of India, Ranchi, Bihar, India, 1974

being, that they likewise make the effort to become divine. Paramahansaji gave this illustration: "In the night sky you see billions and billions of stars and the light they each give to the world. Then look at the moon; one moon gives more light than all the stars. I am looking for those souls who will become mooned personalities, filled with the divine light that is their true nature."

The way to begin to spiritualize one's life is by meditation: the Raja Yoga science of knowing God, which was taught by Bhagavan Krishna in the Bhagavad Gita, and is the same Kriya Yoga science taught by Paramahansaji and his line of gurus. Kriya Yoga is at once simple and yet profoundly effective in spiritualizing man's whole being and bringing it into harmony with God.

WE CAN CHANGE THE WORLD
BY CHANGING OURSELVES

Man is harassed, unhappy, worried, tossed about by the constant change and turmoil of this world. The unending variety of upsets and unrest causes great pain and sorrow in the life of everyone in every country the world around. The ills of society and the world will not be cured by conferences and talk of cooperation and peace if the very persons at the negotiating table have not the peace of true selflessness in their hearts. Nor will peace and prosperity be brought about merely by legislation. The more laws man will make, the more fun miscreants will have in breaking them. The only way this world will change, the only way man is going to be freed from this misery and disturbance, which is day by day poisoning his life and happiness in a slow death of disillusionment, is when he, as an individual, will change himself. At least for a little time each day he must try to pierce the veils of change and *maya,* delusion, and glimpse the Divine Creator, and the purpose of His creation and of each individual human life. This can be done only in the stillness of meditation, if for only five minutes, thirty minutes, an hour a day. Is one hour out of the twenty-four too much to give to God? Is it too much to give to the pursuit of everlasting happiness?

Who are the truly happy, peaceful people in this world? They are not likely to be found among the materially rich or powerful, or among ordinary human beings, who settle for a little temporary pleasure in the fulfillment of some material desire. The truly contented are the saints and sages: They have learned to create, right within themselves, a kingdom of happiness, a fortress of unshakable peace and security, a temple of divine communion at the feet of God. To die to this world for a little while each day — in deep communion with God, through meditation — is to begin to change oneself within.

Then the tiny light of one's life grows brighter and brighter, until he, like the saints, becomes a moonèd personality. Wherever a saint goes, people draw around him, and are influenced toward good, because they feel at least momentarily a little happiness, security, and contentment soothing their troubled beings. When more and more souls will take up this spiritual call of God, *then* our world will begin to change for the better.

India Blessed With Divine Souls

In India you find some of the most beautiful saintly examples. This nation has been blessed as no other with souls who are manifestations of divinity, examples of how we too are to live and to govern our lives, our family, our community, our nation, our world. We have seen how one humble devotee of God, one deep lover of God and of all humanity —Mahatma Gandhi — was able to free this great nation solely by divine love and by the sheer force of goodness, which gave power to his will and to his frail body.

We can tell you, coming from the West, having studied and lived a part of its history, that the great error of the Western world was and is that it has pinned too much of its hope for security and happiness on material gain. But wealth in itself has not proved sufficient to make this world a better place. Creating more comforts for the satisfaction of the senses, fulfilling a few material desires, is not enough. Whenever people begin to exclude God from their hearts, and from their daily lives and aspirations, they are surely headed toward dire difficulties.

The Divine Mother does not want to punish Her

children. She is the One most deeply hurt when they suffer. She cries: "My children, can you not see? Are you so blind? I have set My laws before you in the scriptures; I have spoken of them through the voices of My saints. I have told you how you must behave in this world if you are going to have prosperity of body, of mind, and of spirit. I have placed Myself before you in countless ways. I have cried to you to listen to My counsel. If you shut Me out, I will not be able to stay My law. It will cause you pain and suffering — not to hurt you, but that you might be awakened from delusion, brought back to your spiritual senses; that you might realize how you *must* behave in My creation."

GOD HAS ALWAYS DWELLED WITHIN US

From all who would call him guru, Paramahansa Yoganandaji asked no less than their utmost effort to change themselves from deluded mortals to awakened children of God. That is why, in translating the name of Yogoda Satsanga Society for the West, he called it Self-Realization Fellowship. He said: "Self-realization is the knowing in body, mind, and soul, that we are one with the omnipresence of God; that we do not have to pray that it come to us; that we are not merely near it at all times, but that God's omnipresence is our omnipresence: that we are just as much a part of Him now as we ever will be. All we have to do is to improve our knowing."

The way to this realization is through meditation, through the Kriya Yoga *sadhana* given to us by the great Gurus of this path. Further defining our name, Paramahansaji said: "Fellowship" stands for "fellowship with God through Self-realization, and friendship with all truth seeking souls"—the brotherhood of man under the Fatherhood of the one God. Self-realization is the divine inner awakening to the truth that we are made in the image of God; that He dwells within us, and has always dwelled within us. He is the essence of our being: *Tat twam asi,* "Thou art That."

But if God is in each individual human life, wherein is He expressed? Can the unkindness and falsehood in man's speech be His? Can man's possessiveness, which divides family from family, community from community, nation from nation, be His? Is His the ugliness in man's face when he frowns on a fellow being because he is of a different race, color, caste, or creed? No, these are not expressions of the Divine One. These are not the image of God in man. But that image is there. Our Guru has told us: "Bring it forth!"

WAKE UP IN GOD!

We have to change ourselves because we *have* to change this world. It is not going to be possible for any human being to survive if man continues in his present trend. God is not pleased when man denies Him a place in His own creation. Unless man becomes more spiritual, unless God and

God's divine laws, principles, and ideals are brought back into this world, the forces that are drawing humanity into conflict, one with another, will destroy man and his world. It is no longer a question of "Shall we?" It has become a case of "We must." We must change ourselves, that we may change our world.

This is the message of Yogoda Satsanga Society of India/Self-Realization Fellowship — the clarion call of God Himself appealing to each of His children: It *is* possible, here and now, to make a divine kingdom of God within yourself. And as our Guru said so beautifully: "Finding God within, you will find Him without, in all peoples and in all conditions." You will see Him behind the beauties of nature; you will see Him expressed in the love, kindness, understanding, and goodness in people. You will see Him also behind all the difficulties and troubles of life. You will realize they are His guiding, sometimes disciplining hand, trying to show you right from wrong, so that you may find the lasting happiness and fulfillment you are seeking.

PART V

THE NEW HUMANITY

Security in a World of Change

*Undreamed-of Possibilities: The Divine
Potentials of All Humankind*

A Forerunner of the New Race

Change yourself and you have done your part in changing the world. Every individual must change his own life if he wants to live in a peaceful world. The world cannot become peaceful unless and until you yourself begin to work toward peace.

—Paramahansa Yogananda

SECURITY IN A WORLD OF CHANGE

BY SRI DAYA MATA

How marvelously far ahead of his time Parama-hansa Yogananda was! Recently I read an article about the controversy as to what we should call God: Are we to say "He," "She," "That," or use some other form of address? Many years ago, when Paramahansaji first came to this country, and even before, he addressed his prayers to: "Heavenly Father, Mother, Friend, Beloved God...." This encompasses all the various love relationships known to humankind. That Divine Being is our Father and also our Mother, our Friend, and our Beloved.

In the ultimate sense, you and I are neither man or woman, masculine or feminine. We are the transcendent soul, which knows no gender identification and only temporarily resides in a male or female form. Each of us is a part of God, endowed with all the qualities that flow from the Divine Being. So let us not be too much concerned as to

Condensed from a talk given in Los Angeles, December 14, 1980. The complete talk is available on videocassette from Self-Realization Fellowship.

whether we call God "Him" or "Her"; let us be more concerned with striving to exemplify godly ideals — eternal and universal love, compassion, kindness, wisdom — all of those qualities that are ideal in the feminine and those that are ideal in the masculine.

I was born in a female body, but I find it very difficult to think either as man or as woman, because I know I am the soul, and so are all of you. Genuine equality springs from the soul; that is what we should focus on. In the sight of God, the two sexes are equal: Both are needed for life to go on; both possess attributes that are absolutely necessary for us to become balanced human beings. We should cultivate in ourselves a combination of masculine and feminine qualities. We need the tenderness and compassion that tend to be predominant in woman, as well as the reason and "go get 'em" spirit usually more evident in man.

Many years ago Leopold Stokowski, the famous symphony conductor and musician who was a devout follower of Paramahansaji, spoke to me while our Guru was in India. "There is something in Paramahansa Yogananda that I have admired ever since I first met him," he said, "and I would like so much to strive for that in myself."

"What is it?" I asked.

He replied, "He has the perfect balance between the qualities of male and female. You cannot think of him as man; you cannot think of him as woman. There is such a marvelous blend of compassion and love with wisdom and strength — those qualities that all of us should express."

If you study any great spiritual figure, certainly the Lord Jesus Christ, do you not see in their lives this perfect blend of masculine and feminine? God has given each one of us those qualities, and it is for us to bring them to the fore in our own personality.

Finding Courage in Times of Darkness

So many people have written to me or come to see me with this concern uppermost in their minds: "We are going through some of the darkest times known in the history of man." To a degree that is true; this is a very troubled period. But I think perhaps we overemphasize this. It can be harmful, because it discourages us and fills us with fear. And no human being should go through life with fear in his heart.

The problems we face today have not been created by God, my dears. They are the result of many years of wrong behavior, improper actions by humanity as a whole. And what humanity sows, that also must it reap.

Now we have come to a crossroads. We can either turn toward self-destruction, which is a very real possibility with the nuclear bombs and other instruments of war we have created. Or we can turn toward a higher life of bringing God back into our lives, following moral values and spiritual ideals by striving to walk in the footsteps of divine ones such as Jesus Christ, Bhagavan Krishna, Lord Buddha, and others. That choice is with us now. This is the period where we must set our course: either toward chaos and destruction, or toward concentration on the divine ideals universally advocated in the great religions, by which we can save ourselves and our world.

As I have mentioned on other occasions, in 1963, when I visited Mahavatar Babaji's cave in the Himalayas, I had a superconscious experience in which I was shown what the world is going through now. That vision ended in victory for good. I hope this will be encouraging to all of you: The darkness will be dispelled, as humanity does its part to live by God's laws of goodness and morality.

The tragic happenings, the senseless violence we see taking place in all countries — there seems to be no reason for it. But there is. Primarily, we have gotten away from our true relationship with God and from actual communion with Him. People feel there is no reason not to vent their bitter feelings on other human beings: "All we need is a gun, and that will take care of our problems." This can never be, for as Christ said, "All they that take the sword shall perish with the sword."

BE A BEACON OF FAITH AND UNSELFISH GIVING TO OTHERS

We must cultivate more faith in the Divine Beloved. That is how to begin on the divine path that will lead us to greater peace and contentment, greater success and deeper communion with God. Start by believing in Him and trusting that He will help you to fulfill your needs. Cling to Him and to the thought, "I know He will not fail me." Go on saying and believing it, while doing the best you can to succeed in all you want to accomplish every day — materially and spiritually.

The next step on the path to a higher life is: Learn to be a giver rather than a taker. The people who are happiest in this world are those who are doing for others — for their family, their neighbors, their community and country. Giving doesn't necessarily mean money or material things. It means also to give a positive word — encouragement to someone who needs support. It means to give kindness and understanding. It means taking the time with our children to give them loving understanding and guidance, and discipline when they need it.

INSTILL SPIRITUAL VALUES IN YOUR CHILDREN

Why have children today gone astray? Children need guidance. If you put a seedling in the earth, in order for it to become a strong, healthy plant you have to tend its growth — surrounding it with a little fence, supporting it with posts or tying it with string so it will grow straight. Otherwise, it may grow awry. Parents have a God-given responsibility to teach and guide their children, from the

earliest age. These truths people seem to have forgotten; these are the failures that have contributed
so much to today's problems.

Take time to talk to your children. Take time to
give them understanding. Take time to listen, rather
than saying, "Don't bother me. I don't have time
now." Help them to feel that they can ask you anything. Help them to cultivate a sense of responsibility, within limits that are appropriate to their age.
Avoid putting unreasonable expectations on your
children. But teach them to have faith in God. Talk to
them about God and how much He loves them, and
about those things that are really important in life —
being truthful, being unselfish, doing one's duty.

Punishment may be necessary occasionally to impress an important lesson. But don't be the kind of
parent that scolds or spanks the child simply because
you are feeling cross; then you are only taking your
own anger out on the child. Remain calm and try to
help them to understand. Explain to them why they
should carry out their duties, and the benefits to
themselves and others. Teach them that what we do,
what we give, comes back to us. There is a tendency
either to be too lenient with children or too harsh;
strike the happy balance. Do unto the child, in other
words, as you would want done unto you.

DWELL MORE IN THE THOUGHT OF GOD

Above all, we need to dwell more in the
thought of God. What does this bring to our lives?

I can only tell you that when I have my meditations every morning and night I feel such sweet love pouring over my soul, it is difficult to hold back the tears. And one thought overwhelms me: "O God, if the whole world could just feel this love! How beautiful, how sustaining it is!" I want this for all of you. I want this for all of humanity.

It has to begin with your own effort to cultivate a relationship with Him. No amount of reading books or talking about God is going to give it to you. If each one of you will promise that from this day forward you will never leave your home in the morning or go to sleep at night unless and until you have given at least fifteen minutes to God — praying, meditating, talking with Him, crying to Him — that is what will bring the experience of the Divine. Never give up, even if there is no response. That is His test. "My child," He says, "are you wanting Me, or are you praying because you want something from Me? Which is it?" How beautiful it is when the devotee can say: "Lord, I don't want anything from You. I only know that what satisfies me is to drink deep of the waters of love and wisdom that You pour into this soul. Give me whatever You think I need."

"Seek ye first the kingdom of God, and His righteousness, and all things shall be added unto you." I made up my mind many years ago as a young girl that I was going to take this one truth from Scripture and either prove it right or prove it false. Now I know, from my own experience: It works.

These are the thoughts to live with every day: "I

love You, God. I need You. Only when You are with
me do I feel peace in my heart. And only when I feel
peace in my heart am I able to convey it to others."
When you have that, then you can conquer the world.

THE REAL VICTORY LIES IN
CONQUERING YOURSELF

"There is a way to conquer life," Paramahansaji
said. "The real victory consists in conquering yourself....If your mental attitude changes constantly under the pressure of tests, you are losing the battle of
life....He who is undefeated within is a truly victorious person." I recorded those thoughts years ago.
The perceptions our Guru expressed are so sublime.
He lived in a world of divine consciousness; there is
a wealth of wisdom in his words to guide us on the
path to a higher, better era of spiritual living.

"I see so much unkindness in the world," said
Paramahansaji, "and there is no excuse for me to
add to it. When you love God, and when you see
God in every soul, you cannot be mean." Think of
this the next time you feel resentment toward someone. Take your mind away from that resentment
and try to think: "But my God is in that soul. The
One that I love, that I say I love, is in that soul. I cannot hate, I cannot be unkind to that soul — although
I may not approve of how the ego impinged upon
that soul is behaving toward me. Still, I can honor
my God in that being." That is how Christ could say
of those who were destroying his body: "Father, for-

give them; for they know not what they do." Isn't it amazing that he could feel this? It was because he saw the soul, the image of God, in all of them.

That was an expression of divinity, of the eternal truths that will endure until the last dawn of life. Kindness, love, honesty, sincerity, compassion — these principles will remain the same for all the ages to come. Words and modes of expression may change, but divine ideals are eternal.

Paramahansaji went on to say: "If someone behaves hurtfully toward you, think of the best ways to behave lovingly toward him. And if he still refuses to be considerate, remain withdrawn for a time. Keep your kindness locked up within, but let no demonstration of unkindness mar your behavior. One of the greatest victories over the little self is to be sure of your capacity to be always thoughtful and loving, to be secure in the knowledge that no one can make you act differently."

So often when someone injures us, there is the desire to strike back or to be mean. To me, the ugliest quality in any human being is that of meanness. It is an insult to the soul, because it shows such smallness. Never be mean; always be large-hearted. Strive always to manifest those qualities about which we read in the lives of the divine ones.

YOUR DUTY: TO CHANGE YOURSELF

"Your important duty," Paramahansaji said, "is to watch yourself, correct yourself; do your best."

Don't make excuses for your flaws. It is very difficult to see our own blemishes. The poet Robert
Burns said it many years ago: "O would some
Power the giftie gie us, to see ourselves as others
see us!" How do we develop that marvelous self-
knowledge for self-improvement? Our Guru taught
us to keep a mental diary, to spend a few minutes
each day in introspection. This is referred to in the
first verse of the Bhagavad Gita, which says (meta-
phorically): "Gathered together on the battlefield
of my body and mind are my good and my evil
tendencies. How did they fare this day? Which had
the victory?" Keeping a mental diary means we ask
ourselves, "How did I behave this day? Was I nasty?
Or dishonest? Was I unkind? How did I respond to
others?" In this way we begin to know ourselves.
And if we see within ourselves things that are not
very attractive, these should not make us despon-
dent. Rather let them motivate us to make a
greater effort to express those positive qualities
that we admire. Take little steps, Paramahansaji
used to say, before you try to take giant steps.

"Because you don't analyze yourself," said
Paramahansaji, "you remain always psychological
furniture, never changing." We do not want to be
psychological antiques. Try to sit on an antique
chair and it breaks. Let us be pliable, always ready
to reform ourselves the moment we see that it is
necessary to do so. Some will say, "Well, I'm too
old to change." Nonsense! Victory is not condi-
tioned by age. As long as there is life, there is an

opportunity to change. As long as there is persistence and an earnest desire, anyone can change.

"When you analyze yourself each night, be watchful that you are not becoming stagnant. You become stagnant when you let circumstances override your better judgment....You dwell too much on petty things, and have no time to think about God." Oh, how true that is! One of the marvelous disciplines of our Guru was that he never permitted us to dwell on pettiness. Why let your mind get bogged down in little annoyances that you allow to upset you? Do not waste your time and energy that way. If you pour water on a duck's back, it doesn't soak the feathers, does it? It just slides right off. So we must be that way with all the inconsequential things of life. Do not react to everything that happens. "Be thou of even mind," as Lord Krishna advised.

"I am part of this world drama," Paramahansaji stated, "and I am apart from it." He taught us to be in the world but not of it. Yes, we have our duties here, but let us not become overly absorbed in material pursuits at the cost of our spiritual well-being. Analyze your life; you can see when you are getting too drugged by the things of this world. How can you extricate yourself? Give more thought to God. Let Him become, as our Guru taught us, the Polestar of your life, around which your thoughts constantly revolve.

I have lived my life that way, and I pray I may live that way to the last breath within me. Without that consciousness I could not go on; the whole mind must be immersed in my Divine Beloved, no matter what happens outwardly. Life is not easy, I admit; it has its crosses. But to carry them with faith, with strength, and with a sense of, "Lord, You are with me. I am all right"—that is the way to live in this world. Only then can we hope for positive change in society, through changing our own lives first. It comes not by our words, my dears, but by our deeds.

The Power of Prayer for World Upliftment

Years ago, when I first came to the ashram, Paramahansaji taught us at the close of our meditations to pray for others. Having communed with God, we put aside thought of self and deeply prayed for all humanity. This was the beginning of our Worldwide Prayer Circle, which has since become a united endeavor of thousands of members and friends who pray deeply, sending a healing force of concentrated thought to all those in need.

Thought has tremendous power. From thought all action springs. Everything in this finite world results from thought. It is the most potent force in the universe, with the power to affect lives, communities, and nations. How important it is, therefore, that our thoughts be positive rather than negative. There are millions of people today who are thinking and acting in a negative way. So it is in the interest of ourselves and our whole planet that we all take an active part in praying for our fellow beings. When enough souls participate, their combined thought-vibrations of goodness, love, compassion, and positive behavior generate a mighty force, which has the power to change lives all over the world.

So I urge all of you this evening, and all those who may hear my voice in the future, to join in this worldwide circle of prayer, of God-communion, that we might contribute our part toward changing the course man seems bent on taking. We can do it. One voice, the voice of Christ, which spoke centuries ago, whose divine message was picked up by a handful of disciples, who passed it on to other disciples, and so on down through two thousand years — that one voice was able to transform the lives of millions. Shall we not join his voice and the voice of our Guru and the teachers and saintly souls of all religions, and contribute toward uplifting this world? We can and we must. We must have the faith to believe that it can be done. I know that it can. But I tell you that each one of you has to do your part. Simply to hear or read these words has no meaning. My hope is to touch the very core of your being with this thought: Change your lives by following the simple suggestions given by Paramahansaji for bringing God into your heart and mind. And join every day in this vast, loosely knitted but strong family of individuals praying for the well-being of the world and everyone in it.

Let God Use You to Bring
His Love to Others

Many years ago I recorded these words of
Paramahansa Yogananda: "Christ came at a critical
time in history, when the world was sorely in need
of spiritual hope and regeneration. His message was
not intended to foster multifarious sects, each claim-
ing him as their own. His was a universal message
of unity, one of the grandest ever given....Jesus as-
sured the downtrodden, the white and the dark
man, the Oriental and the Occidental, that they are
all children of God; whoever is pure in heart, no
matter what his race or color, can receive the
Lord."* May we all remember his teaching, and in a
more sincere and dedicated way try to live it.

Pray that God use you to bring His love to others. Now, this does not mean He is instantly going
to convert you into a spiritual teacher. So many people want to be great teachers. I don't know why. I
want to be a great devotee, a great lover of my
Divine Beloved. I want to be among the greatest
lovers of God that the world has ever known. I have
a long way to go, perhaps many lives, but that is my
goal. I have none other, because in that love I find
all that I have ever wanted in this life, or could possibly want in any life. I want to be so drunk with the
love of my Beloved that I know nothing but that

* "But as many as received him [the Christ Consciousness manifested
in Jesus and in all creation], to them gave he power to become the sons
of God" (John 1:14).

love — and by the example of my life arouse in others the same longing to be in love with Him.

This ideal of divine love took birth within me at the feet of that Christlike being, Paramahansa Yogananda. He lived and walked and moved in that consciousness of God as his Beloved. I saw that no matter what he was dealing with — guiding the lives of disciples who had come to him for spiritual help, looking after the mundane cares of this society, persevering even in the face of persecution and non-understanding in the establishment of this pioneering spiritual work — he never let his mind waver from God, the Divine Polestar of his life.

HARMONIZING OUR INNER
AND OUTER LIVES

The lesson we are to learn on this earth is to harmonize our outward duties with our search for God. As Paramahansaji said, "If you are busy for God, then no matter what tasks you are performing, your mind will be always on Him. You should not neglect God for work, and you should not neglect work for God." It isn't difficult, dear ones. I saw our Guru do it; I do it. My responsibilities are more than many have, but I don't let anything take the place of my God. He is the sustainer of my being and He is the sustainer of yours. Put God first.

All that is needed is to sit quietly for just ten to thirty minutes or longer every day and free the mind from restless disturbing thoughts and worries about our lives, our children, our finances and health. Shut it all out! One day the Divine is going to snatch us away from this world and all our responsibilities and preoccupations here. We will not have a chance to think of any of that. While we can, let us take time to commune with Him. If you do this each day, you will find that in mysterious ways something comes into your life that begins to brighten your path, to give you more understanding and greater calmness with which to recognize opportunities and deal with problems.

In the secret chamber within, quietly talk to Him: "My God, my God...." Even when you are with other people, as you are listening to them you can still be feeling within, "I love You, Lord. I love You." Doesn't the lover think that way when he is in love with someone, wherever he is? Doesn't the mother feel that way about her newborn baby? No matter what she is doing, her mind is thinking of her little baby, so sweet and pure. That's the way the devotee thinks of God. Cultivate that loving relationship. It is not difficult. Make the effort. And the more you make the effort, the more that Presence will become a reality to you.

"Meditate every day," Paramahansaji said, "and be thinking of God as you carry your heavy bag of worldly duties." In God is the strength we need to carry out our duties, which are assigned to us as a part of our earthly schooling. And when He decides that we do not need a particular assignment anymore, He will lift that burden from us. And He will give us another one, no doubt! But He will also give us equal strength to deal with it. God would not give the cross of Christ to a little child to carry. He gave that to one who was able to bear it. We never receive any burden that is greater than our ability to carry. But He brings us just to the point where we think we can't carry our load, because that is the way we strengthen our spiritual muscles.

If you want to increase your strength, it won't help to exercise with tiddly-winks. But if you lift a five- or ten-pound rock, then your muscles are getting some exercise! So whenever a burden comes in your life, know that the Lord purposely has not given you a tiny pebble to carry, but something to strengthen your faith and determination — a chance to develop this marvelous machine, the mind, whose full capacity has hardly been tapped. Such tremendous power is in our minds; science has not yet plumbed its depths. That power will be fully expressed only when we reach Christ consciousness, when we become united with the Divine Beloved.

SECURITY LIES IN THE CONSCIOUSNESS OF GOD'S PRESENCE

"I live in the glory of that consciousness of His presence every day," Paramahansaji said. "I feel a wonderful detachment from everything else." That is the state that we eventually come to. This does not mean that we do not care about anything. We do care — and in fact, because we are not attached to anything, we enjoy everything more fully.

"Spirit is my food; Spirit is my joy; Spirit is my feeling, Spirit is my temple and my audience; Spirit is my library, whence I draw inspiration; Spirit is my love and my Beloved. The spirit of God is the satisfier of all my desires, for in Him I find all wisdom, all the love of a beloved, all beauty, all everything.... Whatever I sought, I found in Him. So will you find."

What security we will find in that consciousness! My dears, God has promised that to every one of us, without exception. Waste no more time. True lovers of God are those who have one wish: "I love my God; and whoever crosses my path, let me rouse God's love in that soul." Live your life in that consciousness, and you will find that this world holds no fear, no darkness for you. And you will be contributing in the highest way to the upliftment of all humanity into a better, more spiritual age.

Can we just for a few moments meditate together? Forget that anyone else exists in this world; feel that you are standing in the center of eternity — alone with the Divine from whom you have sprung, only God and you. Pray to Him, in the language of your soul, that He fulfill your deepest yearnings: for peace, for happiness and love, for the unshakable security of His presence in which no trouble or fear of this mortal realm can ever intrude. Be filled with the light of that Eternal Presence, and send out prayerful thoughts of divine love — of peace on earth and goodwill toward all humanity.

May God bless you all.

Undreamed-of Possibilities:

The Divine Potentials
of All Humankind

By Brother Mitrananda

We would like to welcome you to the first in a series of lectures on the life and teachings of our founder, Paramahansa Yogananda. I don't know how much you may know about the science of Yoga that Paramahansaji taught, but I am sure you are more familiar with the term than most participants at the first Parliament of Religions, held here in Chicago 100 years ago. Even twenty-seven years later in 1920, when Paramahansaji arrived in America, Yoga was little known in the West.

It is an interesting "coincidence" that 1993 marks not only the hundredth anniversary of that first Parliament but also the birth centennial of Paramahansa Yogananda. The year 1893 was actu-

Extracts from a talk given at Parliament of the World's Religions, Chicago, August 31, 1993

ally a pivotal one in world and religious history—
the beginning of the awakening in the West of an
interest in the ancient spiritual science of the East;
the beginning, in one sense, of a global spirituality. I say this because the single most prominent
name to come out of that 1893 Parliament was
that of Swami Vivekananda, whose appearance
there marked the first time a great spiritual teacher
of India had come to the West.

We are hearing him mentioned again and again
this week, yet most people are probably unaware
that at the 1893 Parliament he was invited only at
the last minute. He was virtually unknown, and because he hadn't been scheduled he was the last
major speaker to make a presentation. In those
days most people read their entire speeches word
for word from prepared texts. Perhaps you've seen
on display that large photograph of the first Parliament with those very old-fashioned-looking,
bearded clerics from the West, who read what
were no doubt very formal speeches. Then Swami
Vivekananda walked up to the podium without a
single note, and with a radiant smile said: "Sisters
and brothers of America." The audience rose to
their feet and gave him a standing ovation before
he even began his talk. Such is the power of love.

When Paramahansa Yogananda came to this
country in 1920, it was that same power of divine
love that touched people everywhere he went....
Two things impressed people: one was the depth
and beauty of his teaching of Yoga, but just as im-

portant was the power of his personal presence, his tremendous aura of love. There was a well-known journalist who has written many books and worked for several major newspapers. He was a presidential attaché, had private audiences with popes, and interviewed more political figures than he could even remember. But when he met Yogananda, he was simply unprepared for what he encountered. "I came to Swami Yogananda with a skeptical mind," he said. "But he gave me not philosophy, not religion, but unconditional love."

That's the essence of what we are all seeking, isn't it? It is the goal not only of religion, but of life. You can take all human needs and desires, put them into a pot and boil them down, and you are left with the one thing we all want: Love.

Paramahansa Yogananda's great love — for God and for his fellow beings — was what enabled him to transcend all barriers. People didn't think of him just as a religious figure. He didn't ask people to follow him. He came to them; he greeted them at their level. He spoke everybody's language. When he was in Washington, D.C., in 1927, he was invited to the White House to meet the President of the United States, Calvin Coolidge, who was famous for his extreme reserve. One story is told of a woman who sat next to "Silent Cal," as he was called, at dinner one time. "Mr. President," she said, "I've just made a bet that I could get three words out of you." He looked at her and said, "You lose." But when Paramahansaji was there, Coolidge let go of his customary reserve. And the day after their meeting there was a little story in one of the Washington newspapers with the headline, "The Man Who Made the President Smile." Paramahan-saji always related to people at a level deeper than their outer roles and positions. He didn't see the President of the United States; he saw a soul.

TOWARD WORLD UNITY AND FELLOWSHIP

It is that spirit of friendship, that respect for one another as souls, that is so inspiring to see at this Parliament of the World's Religions. The deep sincerity with which so many representatives of such diverse paths are coming together in friend-ship makes a powerful impression on us all, and we see more than ever that this example of unity and fellowship is truly what religion should be up-holding for the people of the world....

That is also why such a beautiful family spirit permeates conferences like this one, because we intuitively recognize each other as fellow seekers. We may not understand exactly what everyone else believes, but it doesn't matter; somehow we know that we are all heading for the same goal.

Paramahansa Yogananda reminded us, as have other spiritual leaders of universal outlook and un-derstanding, that there are many paths to that goal, but underlying them all there is one Truth. Whether we observe one kind of ritual or another, whether we use this name or that name for the object of our worship, is not important. These are the superficial aspects, which differentiate one religion from another in the outer sense. We don't need to be divided over these issues; they simply reflect the wonderful international diversity that characterizes the spiritual quest that is life.

Here at the Parliament we see representatives from 400 different faiths. It is somewhat ironic, because there are not 400 Gods, are there? And yet that is the richness and charm of our global family: We see here people in such different costumes, coming from so many different places in the world. If we all thought alike, worshiped alike, and dressed alike, life would be dull, and we wouldn't appreciate one another as much. But underlying this diversity is a divine unity. Paramahansaji came to show that universal oneness of truth — particularly between original Christianity as taught by Jesus Christ and original Yoga as taught by Bhagavan Krishna centuries before, and that these principles, in a larger sense, are the unifying foundations of all great religions.

RELIGION MUST SATISFY THE DEEPEST YEARNINGS OF THE SOUL

What people today are seeking in religion is an answer to the instinctive yearnings of the soul. We were all born; we don't know where we came from. We're all going to die; we don't know where we're going. Yet intuitively we know or feel there must be answers, spiritual answers; and our souls won't rest until we find them. As children of God, made in His image, we are haunted creatures. We can't really be satisfied for long with being "one-horsepower individuals," as Paramahansaji used to call those who are stagnant with limited goals, doing little things. We always want more, we are always looking on the horizon; we are driven to find perfection. This is our soul nature struggling to express itself. Each of us is being propelled, by the yearnings and urgings that come from deep within, toward a single goal. In that sense, we are *all* religious; we *all* believe in God, whether or not we use that particular label.

"Many people may doubt that finding God is the purpose of life," Paramahansa Yogananda said, "but everyone can accept the idea that the purpose of life is to find happiness — an inner state of permanent Bliss that no outward circumstance, in life or death, can take away. I say that God is happiness. He is Bliss. He is Love. He is Joy that will never go away from your soul." This universally appealing conception of God erases all arguments; it puts religion in terms that are immediately meaningful to the deepest needs and desires of every human being.

Once a radio journalist asked the renowned pianist Arthur Rubinstein if he believed in God. "No," he replied with a twinkle in his eye. "I believe in something much, much greater."

Mahatma Gandhi put it this way: "The time of re-

ligion is over; the time of spirituality has come."
With the power of modern weapons, we see that
we can't afford wars any longer, religious or otherwise. So the issue is being forced on us: one way or
another we have to find that essential commonality,
that unity underlying all humanity. As we do, we
will see more and more this tremendous spirit of
coming together, as we are doing at this Parliament.

What we see happening here transcends neat
intellectual categories, because we are not meeting on the mental plane, where doctrines and dogmas keep us divided, but on the spiritual plane,
where we find common ground because we are
addressing needs and aspirations that are shared
by every human being.

THE DIVINITY OF ALL HUMANKIND

We who are trying to live on the spiritual plane
are what might be called forerunners of a new world
order. Speaking at a conference of the World Fellowship of Faiths in 1937, Paramahansa Yogananda
said: "It is a new world we face, and we must mold
ourselves to the changes. An absolute necessity for
the new generation is the recognition of the divinity of all mankind, and the sweeping away of all
divisive barriers."

Over the past century, our civilization as a
whole has graduated out of a material era into a
mental era; now we need to take the next step, into
the spiritual era. A characteristic of our time has

been an enormous increase in knowledge, in technology, in control over the physical forces of the outer world. But there has not been a corresponding increase in inner control, in self-knowledge and self-discipline. The by-products of scientific and technological achievements have been a tremendous complexity in our lives, a tremendous stress that we have been ill-equipped to handle. We have what are called "complexes," because we lack the spiritual tools to deal with our complex lives. That is why people in this era, perhaps more so than in those of the past, find that Yoga — the science of spirituality — speaks directly to them. They are looking to Yoga not merely because they *want* it, but because they *need* it.

Yoga speaks so effectively to the inherent spiritual needs of humanity because it consists of scientific techniques for putting us in direct communion with God. If you don't like the word *God,* that's fine; it is not a problem. The essence of Yoga is not in semantic labels or dogmas; it simply means "union"— to bind, to yoke together our individual Self or soul with the Source of our being. The word *religion,* which comes from the Latin *religare,* means the same thing: "to bind or bring together."

Paramahansaji named his organization "Self-Realization Fellowship," because, he said, "The real proof of any religion is not out there in the stars. It is within yourself." He often used the illustration of the musk deer in India who runs madly around trying to find the source of this haunting fragrance of musk, and eventually runs right off a cliff, never suspecting that what it was seeking was right within itself. Our situation is similar: We need to be able to sit down and be quiet and hear that still small voice within, and feel that inner peace which is the first proof of God's presence. This is what people are seeking — actual experience.

RELIGION SHOULD BE BASED NOT ON BELIEF BUT ON ACTUAL EXPERIENCE

I grew up in metropolitan Los Angeles, and was raised in a Christian denomination. In the church my family attended, I heard one word used perhaps more than all other spiritual words put together; and that word was *faith*. We need to have *faith* in God, we need to have *faith* that this is how the laws work. Paramahansa Yogananda took the idea of faith a step further, emphasizing that the basis of true faith is not someone else's testimony but one's own experience. "I don't ask you to believe anything I have told you. I ask only that, if you are a sincere seeker, you try these teachings and practice these techniques, so that you may know through your own experience the truth of what I am telling you."

When people would ask Paramahansaji, "What's the difference between your teaching and any other?" he would just say, "Test them." That is what he had done. If you are seeking a path to follow, investigate that which draws your interest. Something will come along that will be more "right" for

you than the others. When you find it, be loyal.
Jump in with both feet and immerse yourself in
whatever teachings you follow, for that is where
you will make the most spiritual progress.

Paramahansa Yogananda respected all paths —
not only respected but loved and deeply appreci-
ated them. He wasn't a competitor; he was a divine friend. He didn't think that he had the only
way, or his was the only important religious society. He was a giver, not a taker. His desire was
only to help, to give love, to encourage, to be a
mother, a father, a friend to all who came. That's
why people responded to him in such an incredible way.

Luther Burbank, the famed horticulturist, was a
great admirer and student of Paramahansa Yogananda. About Yogananda's teachings, he said,
"Through [this] system of physical, mental, and
spiritual unfoldment, by simple and scientific methods of concentration and meditation, most of the
complex problems of life may be solved, and peace
and goodwill shall come upon earth."

Dr. Camille Honig, who was the literary editor
of a magazine called *The California Jewish Voice,*
recounted: "I remember Mahatma Gandhi once
talked to me about Yogananda with great admira-
tion. It is spiritual men like Yogananda who
brought a message of real hope for a deeper understanding between India and the West, perhaps
more than all the politicians put together, he said."

SPIRITUALITY BRINGS A JOY IN LIVING

"All history resolves itself into a biography of a few stout and earnest persons," Ralph Waldo Emerson declared. These are the great ones. They are the ones that change the world, not the economic or political leaders. The saints and the masters outrange them all.

Aside from Paramahansaji's spiritual greatness, what reached so many people on a personal level was his witty, charming, deep, profound, and yet appreciative view of life. He didn't take life so seriously that it was not fun. Isn't that the kind of life we are looking to live? to progress spiritually, and yet to have fun doing it. Paramahansa Yogananda was the living embodiment of that. That's why people of all races, of all nationalities, felt that he embodied what they were searching for. It was as if you could point your finger at this man and say: "That's the goal."

If you go to Europe, you see those magnificent cathedrals with their beautiful paintings and statues of the saints, which are so much a part of the history of Western religion. And yet I was always a little put off by this experience because of the way those artists had portrayed the saints—they always look rather pinched, certainly not very happy! It makes you feel, "Whatever path they followed to get to God, I would like not to go that way!" Some people think that living the spiritual life means a person must be somber and austere, but this is a misconception. If you met a saint in person, you would find that saints are the most happy, loving, uplifting individuals to be around. In hundreds of photographs of Yoganandaji, he is beaming. You see him with anyone, in any situation, and there is a radiance, a joy, that literally flows from his person.

If there is one thing we can say about those who really live the divine life, it is that they are balanced people. They do not live weird or warped lives. Paramahansaji came to teach this balanced, modern approach — one that is livable by anybody, not just those who reside in monasteries or ashrams. That is the power of Yoga: It is a science of living that is universal; and one that is timeless — in recorded history, it is at least six thousand years old. And its fundamental methods and teachings have not changed one iota over all those years.

Meditation Is the Key

I'm sure most of us here have had such an experience, or maybe many of them, which proved to us that we don't have the inner wherewithal to be consistently happy with life unless we have made a connection with God — one that flows from the heart and soul. That is what meditation helps us to establish.

One of our senior monks once commented to me about somebody who was having a difficult time on the spiritual path: "That person does not meditate." I wondered how he could make such a blanket statement without knowing the details of that individual's personal life. So I asked, "How do you know that?" He replied, "He couldn't be meditating. If he were, he would be changing; he would be improving."

It's that simple, because yoga meditation is a science. It conforms to the requirements of science; that is, it consists of actions that can be performed by anyone in any "laboratory" in the world, and the identical result will always obtain. This is the requirement of a science — the results have to be repeatable. The appeal of Yoga is that it works for everyone, limited only by the individual's desire to change, expressed in his or her own efforts at meditation.

One of Paramahansa Yogananda's most advanced disciples was an older woman named Sri Gyanamata, whom he recognized as having been a saint in former lives. She said, "All of Paramahansaji's teachings and techniques have the one end of showing the beauty of holiness. They teach the natural, average man or woman how to become a saint." Through practice of the science of yoga, you can become a saint — that is, someone who knows God. However, it's not easy; patient, determined effort is necessary.

Our goal as sincere yogis is to make every day's meditation deeper than yesterday's, and to make every day's service a little more selfless than that of the day before. This is not mere philosophy; it's a path of action. It works — this is its real power. It

brings what we are all looking for — a personal experience of Truth, of God. We don't want merely
to read about truth. We don't want just to listen to
sermons about it. We want to have that same experience which Christ manifested; that same
knowledge which Buddha possessed; that same radiant joy demonstrated by Lord Krishna. We want
to be Yoganandas; we want to be Vivekanandas.
And it is in the very nature of our souls to evolve,
through self-effort, into that kind of being. That is
the ultimate destiny of every one of us.

"UNDREAMED-OF POSSIBILITIES"

I would like to read to you something that we
quote in our Self-Realization Fellowship literature
when we try to communicate to inquirers something about Yoga's scope and appeal. This quote is
from the Swiss psychiatrist Carl Jung, who said:
"When a religious method recommends itself as
'scientific,' it can be certain of its public in the
West. Yoga fulfills this expectation. Quite apart
from the charm of the new and the fascination of
the half-understood, there is good cause for Yoga
to have many adherents. It offers the possibility of
controllable experience and thus satisfies the scientific need for 'facts'; and, besides this, by reason
of its breadth and depth, its venerable age, its doctrine and method, which include every phase of
life, it promises undreamed-of possibilities."
What is an "undreamed-of possibility"? It is one

that we didn't have the courage to dream, because we were too afraid we would be disappointed yet again, as we have been by so much in this world. In the ultimate sense, the search for God on a scientific basis is the only thing that will never disappoint us, because it is experiential; it changes us, and puts us in tune with the Source of all joy, love, freedom. That scientific search is Yoga, by whatever name you call it.

Victor Hugo said: "The strongest thing in the entire universe—stronger than all the armies, stronger than all the massed might of the world—is an idea whose time has come." I think that's what we sense in the world today, particularly in conferences like this. The time of religion is coming to an end and the time of spirituality has begun. We need a spiritual renaissance, and we are the ones who can bring it—not by changing the world, but by changing ourselves, by teaching through our own example. We don't need to talk about religion; we don't need to talk about philosophy; we don't even need to talk about love. We need to *live* it.

Sri Daya Mata, who was with Yoganandaji for more than twenty years, gave a direct and profoundly simple definition of love when she said, "The secret of love is to give it and not ask for it in return." To give love to God and to our fellow beings: attaining the goal of life is just that simple, isn't it? As we do that, we see that our own needs and aspirations are being fulfilled; everything starts to fall into place. If we can teach our children that, we don't need to teach them anything more. And if we can learn it ourselves, we have mastered the one lesson that we are here on earth to learn.

In closing I would just like to put forth one more thought, an extension of Jung's notion of "undreamed-of possibilities." Paramahansaji used a word that you will seldom see in any magazine or newspaper; and very few people even know what the word means, yet it is the key to success in life. That word is *volition.* It means to adhere to a goal steadily until success is achieved, at any cost, or to die trying. As we make this kind of effort on the spiritual path, we begin to understand another word, which again we don't hear very often. That word is *epiphany.* It's used in the Bible and the old cultures, and we'll hear it more and more in the higher ages. It means an undreamed-of, ecstatic, unlooked-for conclusion. That is what is awaiting us. We look for so much from the outside world, and we hope for so much from other people. But in the end, we will find everything we've been searching for inside ourselves. Yoga is the key that unlocks the door.

A FORERUNNER OF THE NEW RACE

BY TARA MATA

Not long after Tara Mata had met Parama-hansa Yogananda in 1924, she wrote the fol-lowing article about a "man" who was blessed with the experience of cosmic consciousness. Though she humbly avoided identification with the person mentioned, the experiences Tara Mata describes were her own.

Those who have read Dr. R. M. Bucke's *Cos-mic Consciousness* and Edward Carpenter's *Towards Democracy** know that these au-thors believe that cosmic consciousness is a natural faculty of man, and that a future race of men on this earth will be born with this faculty well devel-

---

* Richard Maurice Bucke, a physician, attended Walt Whitman during the latter part of his life, after the great poet had been stricken (in 1873) with paralysis. Dr. Bucke later wrote a biography of Whitman, the first of importance to describe him as a mystical superman; and edited several volumes of Whitman's letters and notes.

The English author Edward Carpenter, after graduation from Cam-bridge, took holy orders and served as a curate in a Cambridge church. He was greatly disturbed by the existing social and religious order, and with the reading in 1868 or 1869 of Whitman's *Leaves of Grass* and *Dem-ocratic Vistas,* his view of life completely changed. Visiting America, he spent some time with Whitman and met Lowell, Emerson, and others. His *Towards Democracy* attracted the attention of many advanced thinkers.

oped, and not merely latent as it is now. Bucke's theory is that, just as man advanced from the state of simple consciousness, which he shared with the animal kingdom, into a state of self-consciousness, peculiar to man alone, and marked by the development of language, so he must inevitably come into a higher state of consciousness, distinguished by a cosmic or universal understanding.

Bucke maintains that the increasing number of people who have attained some degree of cosmic consciousness in the past few centuries is proof that these persons constitute the vanguard or forerunners of the new race. Among those whom Bucke believes to have had the cosmic sense more or less well developed (in recent centuries) are St. John of the Cross, Francis Bacon, Jakob Boehme, Blaise Pascal, Spinoza, Swedenborg, William Blake, William Wordsworth, Alexander Pushkin, Honoré de Balzac, Emerson, Tennyson, Thoreau, Walt Whitman, Edward Carpenter, and Ramakrishna.

Besides these famous men, it is doubtless true that many hundreds of men and women in each century, unknown to fame, have been exalted to some degree of cosmic consciousness. There is no doubt in my mind that the message of Self-Realization Fellowship (founded by Paramahansa Yogananda) in this century has been the means by which hundreds and perhaps thousands of students throughout the world have achieved, through the meditation practices taught them, a glimpse of divine consciousness. Some few students have gone farther and attained very high illumination. Here we have an example of how the cosmic sense is being developed in larger and larger numbers, paving the way for the great race of the future.

One selection from Bucke's book is well worth quoting here:

In contact with the flux of cosmic consciousness all religions known and named today will be melted down. The human soul will be revolutionized. Religion will absolutely dominate the race. It will not be believed and disbelieved.

It will not be a part of life, belonging to certain hours, times, occasions. It will not be in sacred books nor in the mouths of priests. It will not dwell in churches and meetings and forms and days. Its life will not be in prayers, hymns nor discourses. It will not depend on special revelations, on the words of gods who came down to teach, nor on any Bible or Bibles. It will have no mission to save men from their sins or to secure them entrance to heaven. It will not teach a future immortality nor future glories, for immortality and all glory will exist in the here and now. The evidence of immortality will live in every heart as sight in every eye. Doubt of God and of eternal life will be as impossible as is now doubt of existence; the evidence of each will be the same. Religion will govern every minute of every day of all life. Churches, priests, forms, creeds, prayers, all agents, all intermediaries between the individual man and God will be permanently replaced by direct unmistakable intercourse. Sin will no longer exist nor will salvation be desired. Men will not

worry about death or a future, about the kingdom
of heaven, about what may come with and after
the cessation of the life of the present body. Each
soul will feel and know itself to be immortal, will
feel and know that the entire universe with all its
good and with all its beauty is for it and belongs
to it forever. The world peopled by men possessing cosmic consciousness will be as far removed
from the world of today as this is from the world
as it was before the advent of self-consciousness.
...This new race is in the act of being born from
us, and in the near future it will occupy and possess the earth.

A DEFINITE WAY TO CONTACT GOD

The fact that there is a technique, such as Self-
Realization Fellowship teaches, whereby cosmic
consciousness can be attained, is in itself proof that
this higher sense is indeed an inherent faculty of all
men, needing but the necessary training to call it
forth. Most people believe that divine knowledge
comes to only a few chosen ones, and that the average man can approach no nearer to God than his
"faith" will take him. Realization that there is a definite *way* to contact God, a technique usable by all
men in all circumstances, has come as such a liberating shock to a number of Self-Realization students
that they feel they have undergone a new birth.

I have one such case in mind — a man who, as
soon as he had heard the Self-Realization message,
was swept up into cosmic consciousness. He is

the only such person, aside from Paramahansa Yogananda, whom I myself have known, though I have heard or read of a number of other Self-Realization students who have had a more or less similar experience.

This man was possessed of intense religious faith and aspiration. Though well-read in the sacred scriptures of the world, especially those of the Hindus, he knew that this intellectual knowledge was barren and stony; it did not feed the soul-hunger within him. He did not wish merely to read about spiritual food, but to taste it. Under the even tenor of his days there yawned a black abyss of despair — despair that he was worthy of any direct contact with God, since no such experience was given to him. He finally came to doubt, not God, but the possibility that he would ever be able to have more than an intellectual comprehension of Him. This conviction struck at the roots of his life, and made it seem a worthless and meaningless thing.

Into this dark night of his soul came the light of Self-Realization. After attending a few of the public lectures by Paramahansa Yogananda, and before taking the class lessons, this man felt the heavy weight of despair lifting from his heart. Returning to his home one night from the last of the public lectures, he was conscious of a great peace within himself. He felt that in some deep fundamental way, he had become a different person. An impulse urged him to look into a mirror in his room, that he might see the new man. There he

saw, not his own face, but the face of Paramahansa
Yogananda, whose lecture he had attended that
evening. The floodgates of joy broke in his soul;
he was inundated with waves of indescribable ecstasy. Words that had been merely words to him
before — bliss, immortality, eternity, truth, divine
love — became, in the twinkling of an eye, the
core of his being, the essence of his life, the only
possible reality. Realization that these deep, everlasting founts of joy existed in every heart, that
this immortal life underlay all the mortality of humanity, that this eternal, all-inclusive love en-
veloped and supported and guided every particle,
every atom of creation, burst upon him with a
surety, a divine certainty that caused his whole being to pour forth in a flood of praise and gratitude.

He *knew*, not with his mind alone, but with his
heart and soul, with every cell and molecule of his
body. The sublime splendor and joy of this discovery were so vast that he felt that centuries, millenniums, countless eons of suffering were as nothing,
as less than nothing, if by such means this bliss
could be obtained. Sin, sorrow, death — these were
but words now, words without meaning, words
swallowed up by joy as minnows by the seven seas.

PHYSIOLOGICAL CHANGES

He was aware, during this first period of illumination and during the weeks which followed, of a
number of physiological changes within himself.

The most striking was what seemed a rearrangement of molecular structure in his brain, or the opening up of new cell-territory there. Ceaselessly, day and night, he was conscious of this work going on. It seemed as though a kind of electrical drill was boring out new cellular thought-channels. This phenomenon is strong proof of Bucke's theory that cosmic consciousness is a natural faculty of man, for it gives evidence that the brain cells which are connected with this faculty are already present in man, although inactive or non-functioning in the majority of human beings at the present time.

Another important change was felt in his spinal column. The whole spine seemed turned into iron for several weeks, so that, when he sat to meditate on God, he felt anchored forever, able to sit in one place eternally without motion or consciousness of any bodily function. At times an influx of superhuman strength invaded him, and he felt that he was carrying the whole universe on his shoulders. The elixir of life, the nectar of immortality, he felt flowing in his veins as an actual, tangible force. It seemed like a quicksilver, or a sort of electrical, fluid light throughout his body.

During the weeks of his illumination, he felt no need of food or sleep. But he conformed his outward life to the pattern of his household, and ate and slept when his family did. All food seemed pure spirit to him, and in sleep he was pillowed on the "everlasting arms," awakening to a joy past all words, past all powers of description.

He had previously suffered from chronic ca-
tarrh; now his body was purged of all sickness. His
family and friends were aware of a great change in
his appearance and manner; his face shone with a
radiant light; his eyes were pools of joy. Strangers
spoke to him, irresistibly drawn by a strange sym-
pathy; on the streetcar, children would come over
to sit on his lap, asking him to visit them.

The whole universe was to him bathed in a sea
of love; he said to himself many times, "Now at last
I know what *love* is! This is God's love, shaming
the noblest human affection. Eternal love, uncon-
querable love, all-satisfying love!" He knew beyond
all possibility or thought of doubt that Love creates
and sustains the universe, and that all created
things, human or subhuman, were destined to discover this Love, this immortal bliss that was the
very essence of life. He felt his mind expand, his
understanding reach out, endlessly widening,
growing, touching everything in the universe,
binding all things, all thoughts to himself. He was
"center everywhere, circumference nowhere."

THE ATOM-DANCE OF NATURE

The air that he breathed was friendly, intimate,
conscious of life. He felt that all the world was
"home" to him, that he could never feel strange or
alien to any place again; that the mountains, the
sea, the distant lands which he had never seen,
would be as much his own as the home of his boy-

hood. Everywhere he looked, he saw the "atom-dance" of nature; the air was filled with myriad moving pinpricks of light.

During these weeks, he went about his daily duties as usual, but with a hitherto unknown efficiency and speed. Typed papers flew off his machine, completed without error in a fourth of his customary time. Fatigue was unknown to him; his work seemed like child's play, happy and carefree. Conversing in person or over the telephone with his clients, his inward joy covered every action and circumstance with a cosmic significance, for to him these men, this telephone, this table, this voice was God, God manifesting Himself in another of His fascinating disguises.

In the midst of his work, he would suddenly be freshly overwhelmed by the goodness of God who had given him this incredible, unspeakable happiness. His breath would stop completely at such times; the awe which he felt would be accompanied by an absolute stillness within and without. Underlying all his consciousness was a sense of immeasurable and unutterable gratitude; a longing for others to know the joy which lay within them; but most of all, a divine knowledge, past all human comprehension, that all was well with the world, that everything was leading to the goal of cosmic consciousness, immortal bliss.

This state of illumination was present with the man for about two months and then gradually wore away. It has never returned with all its pristine force, though certain features, especially the sense of divine peace and joy, return whenever he practices the Self-Realization meditation techniques.

We can well imagine, with Doctor Bucke, that a race of men, possessing as a normal and permanent faculty this sense of cosmic consciousness, would soon turn the earth into a paradise, a planet fit for Christs and Buddhas, a polestar for the wheeling universe.

EPILOGUE

You are all gods, if you only knew it. Behind the wave of your consciousness is the sea of God's presence. You must look within. Don't concentrate on the little wave of the body with its weaknesses; look beneath. Close your eyes and you see the vast omnipresence before you, everywhere you look. You are in the center of that sphere, and as you lift your consciousness from the body and its experiences, you will find that sphere filled with the great joy and bliss that lights the stars and gives power to the winds and storms. God is the source of all our joys and of all the manifestations in nature....

Awaken yourself from the gloom of ignorance. You have closed your eyes in the sleep of delusion. Awake! Open your eyes and you shall behold the glory of God — the vast vista of God's light spreading over all things. I am telling you to be divine realists, and you will find the answer to all questions in God.

* * *

Periodically throughout its history the world has gotten into a mess. During times of war it becomes a torture chamber for millions of human beings. True happiness, lasting happiness, lies only in God, "having whom no other gain is greater."* In Him is the only safety, the only shelter, the only escape from all our fears. You have no other security in the world, no other freedom. The only true freedom lies in God. So strive deeply to contact Him in meditation morning and night, as well as throughout the day in all work and duties you perform. Yoga teaches that where God is, there is no fear, no sorrow. The successful yogi can stand unshaken midst the crash of breaking worlds; he is secure in the realization: "Lord, where I am, there Thou must come."...

Make the Lord the Shepherd of your soul. Make Him your Searchlight when you move along a shadowy pathway in life. He is your Moon in the night of ignorance. He is your Sun during the wakeful hours. And He is your Polestar on the dark seas of mortal existence. Seek His guidance. The world will go on like this in its ups and downs. Where shall we look for a sense of direction? Not to the prejudices roused within us by our habits and the environmental influences of our families, our country, or the world; but to the guiding voice of Truth within.

***

The only way to know and to live in truth is to develop the power of intuition. Then you will see that life has a meaning, and that no matter what

* Paraphrase of Bhagavad Gita VI:22.

you are doing the inner voice is guiding you. That voice has long been drowned in the mire of untrue thoughts. The surest way to liberate the expression of intuition is by meditation....

Meditate and pray deeply; and wait for His response. If you repeatedly call on Him with ever deeper concentration, He will answer your prayer. A joy and peace will strike your heart. When that comes, you know that you are communing with God....

When you contact God, intuitive perception of truth will guide you in everything you do....Why not consciously attain that Power which never fails you? Realize that Power within yourself....You will find that Power works in everything to make your life complete, your health vibrant with cosmic energy, and your mind keen with the focused clarity of concentration. You will realize that your soul is a receptacle of God's unfailing, ever-guiding truth and wisdom.

God is the Fountain of health, prosperity, wisdom, and eternal joy. We make our life complete by contact with God. Without Him, life is not complete. Give your attention to the Almighty Power that is giving you life and strength and wisdom. Pray that unceasing truth flow into your mind, unceasing strength flow into your body, and unceasing joy flow into your soul. Right behind the darkness of closed eyes are the wondrous forces of the universe, and all the great saints; and the endlessness of the Infinite. Meditate, and you will realize the omnipresent

Absolute Truth and see Its mysterious workings in your life and in all the glories of creation.

* * *

The Hindu scriptures teach that man is attracted to this particular earth to learn, more completely in each successive life, the infinite ways in which the Spirit may be expressed through, and dominant over, material conditions. East and West are learning this great truth in different ways, and should gladly share with each other their discoveries. Beyond all doubt it is pleasing to the Lord when His earth-children struggle to attain a world civilization free from poverty, disease, and soul ignorance. Man's forgetfulness of his divine resources (the result of his misuse of free will) is the root cause of all other forms of suffering.

The ills attributed to an anthropomorphic abstraction called "society" may be laid more realistically at the door of Everyman. Utopia must spring in the private bosom before it can flower in civic virtue, inner reforms leading naturally to outer ones. A man who has reformed himself will reform thousands.

* * *

Distinctions by race or nation are meaningless in the realm of truth, where the only qualification is spiritual fitness to receive.

God is Love; His plan for creation can be rooted

only in love. Does not that simple thought, rather than erudite reasonings, offer solace to the human heart? Every saint who has penetrated to the core of Reality has testified that a divine universal plan exists and that it is beautiful and full of joy.

* * *

Let us pray in our hearts for a League of Souls and a United World. Though we may seem divided by race, creed, color, class, and political prejudices, still, as children of the one God we are able in our souls to feel brotherhood and world unity. May we work for the creation of a United World in which every nation will be a useful part, guided by God through man's enlightened conscience. In our hearts we can all learn to be free from hate and selfishness. Let us pray for harmony among the nations, that they march hand in hand through the gate of a fair new civilization.

About Paramahansa Yogananda

Paramahansa Yogananda (1893–1952) is widely regarded as one of the preeminent spiritual figures of our time. Born in northern India, he came to the United States in 1920, where for more than thirty years he taught India's ancient philosophy and science of yoga meditation and the art of balanced spiritual living. The first great master of Yoga to live and teach in the West for an extended period of time, he traveled and lectured extensively throughout North America and abroad, speaking to capacity audiences in major cities and revealing the underlying unity of the world's great religions. He has inspired millions through his acclaimed life story, *Autobiography of a Yogi,* his groundbreaking commentaries on the scriptures of East and West, and his numerous other books. Paramahansa Yogananda's spiritual and humanitarian work continues to be carried on today by Self-Realization Fellowship, the international society he founded in 1920 to disseminate his teachings worldwide.

Other Contributors

Sri Daya Mata, president of Self-Realization Fellowship/Yogoda Satsanga Society of India, is the foremost living disciple of Paramahansa Yogananda. A true "Mother of Compassion," as her name signifies, she has inspired people from all walks of life with her wisdom and great love of God, cultivated through her own practice of daily meditation and prayer for more than seventy years. She entered the monastic order at the age of seventeen, and in 1955 she became one of the first women in modern history to be appointed head of a worldwide religious movement. As the spiritual leader of Paramahansa Yogananda's work, Daya Mata has made several global speaking tours, and two anthologies of her lectures and informal talks in the U.S. and India have been published: *Only Love: Living the Spiritual Life in a Changing World* and *Finding the Joy Within You: Personal Counsel for God-Centered Living.* A third book, *Enter the Quiet Heart: Creating a Loving Relationship With God,* was published in 1998. Many of her talks are available on audiocassette.

Sri Mrinalini Mata became a monastic in Self-Realization Fellowship in 1946 and has served as vice-president of the society since 1966. Personally instructed by Paramahansa Yogananda in the preparation of his teachings for publication, she has served for many years as editor-in-chief of Self-Realization Fellowship books, lessons, and periodicals. Yogananda's critically acclaimed translation of and commentary on the Bhagavad Gita and three anthologies of his talks are among his works that have been published under her direction. Her talks on a variety of subjects have been published in *Self-Realization* magazine and on audiocassette.

Tara Mata met Paramahansa Yogananda in 1924 and took her final vows as a monastic in 1936. Under the direction of Paramahansa Yogananda, she became editor-in-chief of Self-Realization Fellowship publications and also served on the Board of Directors and as vice-president of the society (1960–1966). She wrote many articles on the science and philosophy of Yoga before her passing in 1971.

Brother Anandamoy came to America from Zurich, Switzerland, in 1948 to study architecture with Frank Lloyd Wright. The following year, impressed by his reading of *Autobiography of a Yogi,* he traveled to Los Angeles to seek out its author. Shortly thereafter he became a monk of Self-Realization Fellowship and was privileged to receive personal guidance and spiritual discipline from Paramahansa Yogananda. Brother Anandamoy has lectured extensively throughout the United States, Europe, and India and is widely regarded as an authority on yoga.

Brother Achalananda has been a Self-Realization Fellowship monk for over forty years, and serves as senior minister at the SRF Lake Shrine in Pacific Palisades, California. He has lectured on the ancient science of yoga and meditation as presented in the teachings of Paramahansa Yogananda throughout North America, Europe, India, Australia, and New Zealand.

Brother Mitrananda serves as a minister at the Self-Realization Fellowship Temple in San Diego, having been a monk for nearly thirty years. He has traveled throughout North America and Europe, lecturing on the teachings of Paramahansa Yogananda.

ALSO BY PARAMAHANSA YOGANANDA

Available at bookstores or directly from the publisher

Autobiography of a Yogi

Autobiography of a Yogi *(Audiobook, read by Ben Kingsley)*

God Talks With Arjuna: The Bhagavad Gita
(A New Translation and Commentary)

The Collected Talks and Essays
Volume I: Man's Eternal Quest
Volume II: The Divine Romance
Volume III: Journey to Self-realization:
Discovering the Gifts of the Soul

Wine of the Mystic: The Rubaiyat of Omar Khayyam —
A Spiritual Interpretation

The Science of Religion

Whispers from Eternity

Songs of the Soul

Sayings of Paramahansa Yogananda

Scientific Healing Affirmations

Where There Is Light: Insight and Inspiration
for Meeting Life's Challenges

In the Sanctuary of the Soul: A Guide to Effective Prayer

Inner Peace: How to Be Calmly Active and Actively Calm

How You Can Talk With God

Metaphysical Meditations

The Law of Success

Cosmic Chants

AUDIO RECORDINGS OF INFORMAL TALKS BY PARAMAHANSA YOGANANDA

Beholding the One in All

Awake in the Cosmic Dream

The Great Light of God

Be a Smile Millionaire

OTHER BOOKS FROM THE SAME PUBLISHER

The Holy Science *by Swami Sri Yukteswar*

Only Love: Living the Spiritual Life in a Changing World
by Sri Daya Mata

Finding the Joy Within You: Personal Counsel
for God-Centered Living
by Sri Daya Mata

God Alone: The Life and Letters of a Saint
by Sri Gyanamata

"Mejda": The Family and the Early Life
of Paramahansa Yogananda *by Sananda Lal Ghosh*

*A complete catalog of books and audio/video recordings
is available on request.*

SELF-REALIZATION FELLOWSHIP LESSONS

The scientific techniques of meditation taught by Parama-hansa Yogananda, including Kriya Yoga — as well as his guidance on all aspects of balanced spiritual living — are taught in the *Self-Realization Fellowship Lessons*. For further information, you are welcome to write for the free booklet, *Undreamed-of Possibilities.*

SELF-REALIZATION FELLOWSHIP
3880 San Rafael Avenue • Los Angeles, CA 90065-3298
TEL (323) 225-2471 • FAX (323) 225-5088
www.yogananda-srf.org